How Shall They Hear?

Maeva Thompson

**Baptist
Publishing
House**

How Shall They Hear?
Baptist Publishing House
ISBN 0-89114-354-8

All Scripture quotations unless otherwise noted are from the *Holy Bible, King James Version.*

Copyright © 2003 by Baptist Publishing House. All rights reserved. No part of this publication may be reproduced or transmitted in any form or by any means, electronic or mechanical, including photocopy, recording, or any information storage and retrieval system, without permission in writing from the publisher. Requests for permission to make copies of any part of the work should be mailed to: Permissions, Baptist Publishing House, Post Office Box 7270, Texarkana, TX 75505-7270.

Printed in the United States of America

Table of Contents

Foreword 5

Preface 6

Acknowledgments 8

How Shall They Hear?

By God's Love 9

By God's Promises 17

By God's Faithfulness 27

By God's Power 34

By God's Grace and Mercy 41

By God's Protection 48

By Our Surrender 56

By Our Obedience 64

By Our Prayer 74

By Our Perseverance 80

By Our Giving 87

By God's Supremacy Over World Conditions 93

"How then shall they call on him in whom they have not believed? and how shall they believe in him of whom they have not heard? and how shall they hear without a preacher? and how shall they preach, except they be sent?" (Romans 10:14-15).

Foreword

How Shall They Hear? These words have been burning in Maeva Thompson's heart since the day she and her missionary parents, Brother and Mrs. James Poole, set foot on foreign soil in Uruguay. Although she was a very young girl, the Lord used the experiences of a few years to motivate her service for years to come. She has such a love for the people of Uruguay and relates that love to people everywhere who need to hear about the saving and sustaining power of our Lord Jesus Christ.

Maeva grew up in a minister's home and then married pastor Ray Thompson and made a godly home of her own for her family. She is a daughter, wife, mother, public school teacher, pastor's wife, teacher for young GMA girls, leader of ladies, a precious friend, and much more. She has unselfishly given her time to promote the Lord's work especially in the area of missions. She has made her home, community, church, and her local, district, state, and national WMA groups the arenas of her service.

Maeva will introduce you to real people who have given their lives to missionary endeavors and to some of the fruits of their labors, unbelievers who became believers and in turn won others. She will also show us that this work is not for just a few specially called people, but that there is a place for every believer to work in this great harvest of souls.

May the study of this book awaken an interest in the reader to pray, support, promote, and participate in carrying out the Great Commission. The results will be that *They Shall Hear!*

Bettye White Wilson

Preface

Several years ago I was asked to give a brief testimony of my experience as a BMAA missionary's daughter in Uruguay during a Missions Symposium worship service. I remember feeling very unworthy to speak, convinced that the testimony should be given by someone else since so many other BMAA missionary children have spent so many more years of childhood than me in far more exotic countries with more unique cultures than my beloved Uruguay.

The Lord gently reminded me that many years before I had made Him a promise. I had promised that I would never refuse to share the truths I learned as a result of one of the most wonderful gifts He has given me, my experience in Uruguay.

As the time approached to give the testimony at the Missions Symposium that December night in Dallas, I was broken in tears in the hotel room. Three things constituted my burden: the fear of being misunderstood, the emotion of my love for the Uruguayan people, and the weight of the awesome responsibility of not wasting this opportunity to share their story.

Jesus filled my heart with His peace that passes all understanding. The Spirit prompted me, "Maeva, just tell My story the way I willed for you to experience it as a child."

Finally, His voice had pierced my frail, human mind. Of course, it's His story, His story, not mine. From that moment I have found deep joy in telling it.

I could not have foreseen in Dallas that night that I would be called upon at a later time to share the story of missions in a form that would require strength and resources far beyond my abilities. This book is a tribute to Philippians 4:13.

The purpose of this book was not to focus upon my personal experience in Uruguay, but rather to challenge the reader to personalize the call that the Lord has placed upon all the saved to go and tell His story.

I thank the Lord for this opportunity and for the deep and abiding joy that still fills my heart daily from my experience on the mission field in Uruguay.

Acknowledgments

To my heavenly Father and my Savior for Your love, Your grace, and Your strength. (Psalm 121).

To my father and mother, James and Allyne Poole, who at midnight on March 21, 1965, stood on either side of me and led me off the ship and into Uruguay, the center of the Lord's will for our lives at that moment, a world of the Lord's amazing grace. With all my heart, I thank you. Some felt you were carrying me away to suffer. To the contrary, you carried me away to sit in heavenly places with precious people whose voices linger with me to inspire and strengthen me daily.

To my family, Ray, Melady, and James Paul, and to my grandmothers who are now with the Lord, Mae Morris and Bernice Poole, and all my extended family for your Christlike love, inspiration, and faithful prayers.

To my brothers and sisters in Christ in Uruguay for your faithful witness in the land we love so much.

To our church family, Enon Baptist Church of Gilmer, Texas, who for thirty years have loved and encouraged us.

To Mrs. Bettye White Wilson for your ministry in my life.

To the Women's Missionary Auxiliary for the joy of serving with each lady.

To the missionaries and their families who contributed the testimonies contained in these pages. May God bless you for your faithful service, for your surrender to the Lord's will, and for the example you set before us.

To Dr. Larry Silvey, Brother Jerome Cooper, and the staff of the Baptist Publishing House for your tireless labor and support.

1

BY GOD'S LOVE

On a balcony of space
    Stepped a pure and holy God.
    And in awesome solitude
He stood alone.
Not one faint star to give Him light,
Just endless rolling, black as night,
But somehow, through the darkness,
He could see.
He saw mountains, high and lofty,
He saw valleys, lush and green,
He saw babbling brooks
And wildflowers growing,
Even heard a robin sing.
Then He felt a strange compassion,
As close to love as pain can be.
Standing out there in His tomorrow,
He saw me.
He saw me in His likeness,
He saw me just like Him,
Clean and pure and holy,
Spotless, white within.
But He saw me bound in heavy chains
And longed to set me free
But He knew if I became like Him,
He must become like me.
Jesus paid it all;
All to Him I owe.
Sin had left a crimson stain;
He washed it white as snow.[1]

The songwriter transports us into a glimpse of God's awesome knowledge and power. She asks us to imagine a scene which our finite minds can barely embrace. She compels us to contemplate a moment in which our Creator stepped out, as it were, onto a balcony of infinity, before space or time or light existed, and in His divine and magnificent mind visualized the creation of everything that exists other than Himself. Only He was present in that moment. In an exercise of His sovereign will, He chose to create for Himself the universe, whose intricate designs and incomparable beauty are testaments to His intellect and power. What could He possibly choose to be the crowning centerpiece of His handiwork that would bring Him the greatest joy and honor? However inconceivable the idea may be to us, the truth is that He chose to make man for that purpose, and then He completed His plan by making woman.

God knew the future entirely, including everything that would transpire in every detail. And yet He eagerly proceeded, knowing what it would cost Him. John captured the reason in one simple statement, *"For God is love"* (1 John 4:8). Because of Who He is, He designed the manner in which redemption for the fallen human soul would be offered. He also laid in place the marching orders by which His plan of redemption would be proclaimed until the end of time. How like God to decide that the plan of salvation would be carried and shared by those who have experienced it! The plan is the gospel message of salvation through Jesus Christ, His Son. The messengers are you and I, who have already been given the unspeakable gift of hearing the plan of salvation, and who have chosen to receive Him into our hearts. Jesus proclaimed to his disciples, *"Ye shall receive power, after that the Holy Ghost is come upon you: and ye shall be witnesses unto me both in Jerusalem, and in all Judaea, and in Samaria, and unto the uttermost part of the earth"* (Acts 1:8).

We have chosen to call our task, our marching orders, by the simple name *missions*. It is impossible to express in the words of any language the gravity or the eternal implications of this word. It is equally impossible to describe the divine love, mercy, and grace that constitute the foundation of this entity we call missions. It is not impossible, however, through God's strength and power, for us to obey the command to be missionaries. What a wonderful privilege! Though we could never hope to repay our salvation, we can present ourselves as instruments in the hands of God to announce to all who will hear that His gift is available. Paul opened his heart to the Romans when he penned the plea, *"I beseech you therefore, brethren, by the mercies of God, that ye present your bodies a living sacrifice, holy, acceptable unto God, which is your reasonable service. And be not conformed to this world: but be ye transformed by the renewing of your mind, that ye may prove what is that good, and acceptable, and perfect, will of God"* (Romans 12:1-2).

Fulfillment in life for every Christian is measured by the degree to which we devote ourselves to this task called missions. We were created for this purpose, because it is by winning souls that we best honor and glorify Him. In so doing we find the joy and peace for which our soul yearns most deeply.

Poets and songwriters have long written about our great need for love. The concept of love has been greatly misunderstood, misinterpreted, and misapplied in individual lives throughout history. Sorrow, pain, tears, injustice, and untold suffering have occurred from the world's distortion of the meaning of love. All of the resulting evil has been born out of human ignorance of the true source of love and the refusal to acknowledge that love is of God, because God is the definition of love.

All pure and true forms of love originate in God's divine love. Any application of love outside of God's design is counterfeit and breeds tragedy. All expressions of love within the will of God are designed to bring about His purpose in the lives of His creation.

The greatest expression of His love was the death of His Son, Jesus Christ, upon the cross to redeem our soul. Our role in the expression of God's love is to be one of action. We must live out His love before people within our reach. We must send His love around the world in the form of the message of salvation. By His love, expressed through us as His instruments, the world will hear the gospel. We must be motivated by His love to recognize that souls await us and we are not promised tomorrow.

The Lord is always aware of the urgency of the witness we present in any given moment. From a village in Mexico comes the perfect illustration of this great truth in the story of a young child called Antonio, shared by missionaries Joe and Belinda Caudle.

Antonio was not the noisiest, nor the handsomest, nor the smartest of the children his age in the small village of Playa Vicente, Veracruz, Mexico. He was known to some people only as "Tito's little brother." But the day arrived that Antonio's name was on the lips of everyone in town. On that day, Antonio was dead at the age of ten.

He had been riding on the bar of his older brother's bicycle on an unpaved rural road. The boys heard a vehicle approaching rapidly from behind. Tito quickly tried to get off the road as far as he could, but his efforts were in vain. The pickup truck was traveling at an uncontrollable speed and hit the bicycle, sending the boys flying into an adjacent field. The pickup driver did not even slow down. A passerby gathered Antonio off the ground, discovering that he was severely injured. His older brother, who had miraculously escaped with hardly a scratch, accompanied the man with Antonio to the small clinic in Playa Vicente where doctors tried desperately to save his life with the limited resources and technology available in rural Mexico. Their efforts were unsuccessful, and Antonio's short life ended that day.

The wake began that evening at the family home, with the grieving brother blaming himself for taking Antonio on the bicycle. The funeral was held promptly the following day, as is customary in Mexico. By law, a body must be buried within twenty-four hours unless embalming occurs. Most people cannot afford this luxury just to prolong the inevitable parting with a loved one. At the funeral most of those attempting to comfort the family had little hope to offer because they themselves had few accurate concepts of life after death. But if Antonio could have returned to speak to them, he would have been able to explain it all.

Just a few days before the accident occurred, Tito invited Antonio to attend Vacation Bible School at the Baptist mission in Playa Vicente. Tito had been attending the mission periodically for a while, and that week he took Antonio to VBS.

As far as religion was concerned, the family of Tito and Antonio followed the common traditions, but were not really active practitioners of their professed religion. One of Antonio's sisters had attended Bible studies conducted by Jehovah's Witnesses, but Tito was the first to appear at the Baptist mission. Their parents seldom attended services at any church and were mostly concerned and busy with the normal affairs of raising a growing family.

When August arrived, Antonio's parents, like many in Playa Vicente, followed the usual pattern of allowing their children to attend VBS. Though they would never have allowed them to attend regular services in the mission, VBS was different because it lasted only one week and provided child care for a few hours each morning. They probably never gave their decision another thought and certainly did not understand what an important invitation Tito had given Antonio.

As usual, the Vacation Bible School was a lively time, with a large group of children gathering to study scriptures, make handcrafts, learn verses, play games, and complete workbooks. Two young men, Bible institute students from El Rinconcito, had arrived to complete an internship. They were assigned as teachers in VBS. Julian, from Tierra Blanca, Veracruz, became the Intermediate class teacher. Pastor, whose name means "shepherd" in Spanish, had been saved under the ministry of Brother and Mrs. Buddy Johnson in Huejutla, Hidalgo. He was assigned as teacher of the Primary class.

Antonio arrived early the first morning of VBS and was placed in Pastor's class. From a cultural perspective, Antonio was probably very impressed with the fact that two young men were participating in religious activities, especially since they helped everyone have so much fun. In Mexico, religion is considered to be mainly for weaker men, women, and children. Most *real* men sit outside the churches on Sunday mornings waiting for their families to emerge so that other Sunday activities can begin. Even on occasions such as funerals or weddings, many men do not attend the ceremonies, but appear for wakes and receptions just in time for the drinking and eating that take place.

To Antonio and the other children, Julian and Pastor were obviously different. They were lively and filled with a joy and enthusiasm for the Bible and the Christian life. Having never seen this before, Antonio must have been as impressed with Julian and Pastor as he was with the Bible lessons, crafts, and other activities of the week.

Like most weeks devoted to VBS, this one passed quickly in a flurry of preparation for the closing program. In the succeeding busy days, no one had found time as yet to compile a list of names of those children who had made professions of faith. Julian and Pastor left to return to the Bible institute.

Soon the fateful afternoon arrived and news of Antonio's death circulated quickly through the town. At the mission, grieving VBS workers attempted to comfort each other. With anxious hearts, they fetched the VBS records and searched the list of those who had prayed the sinner's prayer for salvation, focusing their attention upon one name. There, scrawled in the handwriting of Pastor, they found this precious name, Antonio.

Pastor had indeed, according to the record, counseled and prayed with several of his young charges. In a single eternal moment, lost to our busy world, but etched upon the glorious pages of the Lamb's book of life, Antonio had lifted his tiny hand, knelt beside his committed teacher, and surrendered his life to Jesus. Just days later, his God-given soul leapt from the small lifeless body lying helpless on the sheets of a clinic gurney and soared to his victory in Jesus. Are we as eternally grateful as we should be? Do we pray that there will be other names added to other lists before their window of opportunity is closed? Will we allow the Holy Spirit to burn the name of Antonio into our minds and hearts as a living testimony of what our purpose in life truly is? Will we commit ourselves to reach all who are lost until that wonderful day when Jesus returns, bringing Antonio with him?

Reflect, Discuss & Apply

1. How can you express your thanks to the Lord today for His divine love that provided redemption for all who believe?

2. How can you visualize who you are before the Lord, from whence you have come, and how merciful He has been? Read Psalms 40:2; 46:10.

   _____
   _____
   _____

3. What does this time spent in reflection motivate you to do in order to be the witness God has called you to be?

   _____
   _____
   _____

4. What can you do to change your focus from people's social, physical, or material status to their spiritual status?

   _____
   _____
   _____

5. What steps do you need to take to establish a daily prayer time in which the Lord will give you a greater burden for souls?

   _____
   _____
   _____

---

[1]"He Saw Me," Joan Ewing, copyright © 1993. Landy Ewing Publishing/ASCAP (admin. by ICG). All rights reserved. Used by permission.

2

BY GOD'S PROMISES

Total surrender to the work of missions is a response to the work of the Holy Spirit in the heart of the believer.

Only the Holy Spirit can place the burden for lost souls upon the heart so vividly and so urgently that the believer is willing to become personally involved in sharing the gospel. Satan is perfectly content for the context of missionary work to be worded in terms of ministry to the masses, because in this frame of reference the masses remain nameless and faceless. The gravity and urgency of the need for action is diluted, and believers drift in mediocrity or indifference.

Believers need to begin each day with the realization that multitudes will die without salvation that day. These multitudes, however, are individuals created in the likeness and image of God who will spend eternity in hell. That truth is sobering! The believer must renounce the temptation to prioritize life in terms of pleasure or worldly gain.

Paul admonished the Philippians, *"Let this mind be in you, which was also in Christ Jesus"* (Philippians 2:5). In embracing and developing the mind of Christ, believers will think first, in every acquaintance and encounter, of the spiritual welfare of those we meet. We will incorporate the testimony of our walk with Him into our conversation, our actions, our personal appearance, and our relationships with others. We will seek and pray for opportunities to specifically share the gospel with all whom God brings to us.

We will recognize procrastination for the tool of Satan that it is. How sad it would be to pass up the opportunity to be the Holy Spirit's tool to influence the eternal destiny of a soul, and to know that one day we will answer to God for those souls, because we ignored His leading when He impressed us to speak to someone about salvation.

We will concede no compromise with worldly views which diminish the urgency and importance of salvation. The commission of the church is to win souls. All other activities and endeavors which do not facilitate missions outreach are not primary objectives of the Lord's church.

We will recognize that the missions outreach of our church on the local, district, state, national, and international levels will only be as strong as the daily Christian walk of each individual member. The time has come for a return to a Christlike lifestyle. Without prayer warriors and front-line soldiers who are committed to this concept, the work of missions suffers. Paul issued this call in Ephesians 4.

In His precious and infinite wisdom, God chose to fill the pages of the Bible with promises that are the most reliable element of eternity. His promises address every potential situation we may face in His service and every possible question we might have about the future. Not every detail is given; if so, we would become entangled with mysteries our finite minds could not process. Instead, He made the promises firm, sure, concise, and secure. We can stand upon them, claim them, and proclaim them. They are the very essence of eternal truth.

The most important of all these great promises is that of the beloved verse found in John 3:16. Jesus declared, *"For God so loved the world, that he gave his only begotten Son, that whosoever believeth in him should not perish, but have everlasting life."*

The second is the promise of security. Jesus declared

in John 10:28, *"I give unto them eternal life; and they shall never perish, neither shall any man pluck them out of my hand."* This promise was so important to Jesus that he repeated it in the very next verse.

The third promise is that every human being will have the opportunity to receive this great salvation. Paul wrote to Titus that *"the grace of God that bringeth salvation hath appeared to all men"* (Titus 2:11). Peter declared that *"The Lord is ... not willing that any should perish, but that all should come to repentance"* (2 Peter 3:9). Matthew recorded the words of Jesus in which He proclaimed that, *"this gospel of the kingdom shall be preached in all the world for a witness unto all nations"* (Matthew 24:14).

We go forth to proclaim the message of the gospel knowing that we have been chosen to carry out this great promise. What an incentive to march forward into the fields that are white unto harvest, and to bring to the fold all those who will hear!

Why do we allow Satan to rob us of this excitement? Why do we not pursue the lost soul in the supermarket with the same energy that we rush to load our grocery carts with the bargain items of the day? Why do we not plot opportunities, under the direction of the Holy Spirit, to witness to lost neighbors and acquaintances with the same anticipation that we devote to conversations with friends and family? Why do we not cheer on our team of missionaries across the world with the same constancy and conviction that we shower upon our children's extracurricular activities? The answer lies in the arrangement of priorities in our lives.

God has promised that He will honor our priorities if we align them with His will. His power and might know no bounds in this matter of mission work, if we pray for the burden to be fully placed in our hearts and then respond daily in word and deed.

We can go forth boldly, knowing that the Lord of the

harvest will give the victory in the lives of those to whom we witness. Paul admonished the Corinthians to be *"stedfast, unmoveable, always abounding in the work of the Lord, forasmuch as ye know that your labour is not in vain in the Lord"* (1 Corinthians 15:58).

God promises that when the seed of His Word is planted, it will bring sinners to repentance. This promise has come to pass in the ministries of missionaries throughout the centuries. No village is too small, no home too humble, for the promise of salvation to reach hearts just in time.

A gentle November breeze floated inland off the winding shoreline of the Rio de la Plata, making the leaves rustle just outside Margarita's window. The ever-present smell of smoke drifting from the neighborhood fires filled the air. The rabbits in their cages in front of the porch had been fed. The barrio dogs lifted their voices in chorus signaling that they would be vigilant through the night. Spring was in the air with its everlasting promise of new life.

This Wednesday had been special, since the roof of the church across the road had been completed in the afternoon. Margarita called the family to supper, prepared in the simple room which served as living and dining quarters for her humble family. Grandmother shuffled along more slowly to the table these days and thus was the last to take her seat. Pablo, Margarita's husband, called for all to bow their heads. A simple prayer was offered in gratitude for the meal. Collectively, the family raised their heads in anticipation of the warm food; everyone, that is, except seventeen-year-old José. As his young body slumped forward over the table, his eternal soul slipped into the arms of Jesus. Spring had indeed brought everlasting new life.

The gospel had arrived just in time in José's Uruguayan barrio of Nuevo Paris. Just seventeen months before José succumbed to lung cancer, missionaries

James and Allyne Poole, along with workers in their mission, had contacted his mother, Margarita, on a makeshift soccer field one cold and rainy Saturday afternoon. She was presented the good news of salvation. A few weeks later, in a hospital bed awaiting amputation of a cancerous leg, José gave his heart to Jesus. During the short months of José's earthly walk with the Lord, he was blessed to see aunts, uncles, brothers, sisters, cousins, and lifelong friends come to know Jesus.

A church building for his barrio became an important goal to José. He accompanied the missionary to ask the owner of property located across the street from his home to consider selling a lot on which to build the church building. The owner initially refused to sell. When the Lord changed the owner's heart about the matter, thereby answering José's prayer, he then began to pray to live to see the church building finished. His heart's desire was granted when the roof was completed the afternoon that he died.

José could not have known, however, that his memorial service would be the setting for an event that is critical to the spread of the message of salvation across the world, the surrender of individual lives to ministry. When the sermon was completed, a young man just ten years older than José answered the Lord's call to preach the gospel. Thus, the witness would go forward as the Lord has promised.

The apostle Paul testified in Philippians 1:20-21, *"In nothing I shall be ashamed, but that with all boldness, as always, so now also Christ shall be magnified in my body, whether it be by life, or by death. For to me to live is Christ, and to die is gain."* To be committed to the work of missions is to make the spreading of the gospel the top priority in life, surrendering so totally that the magnifying of Christ to the world is more important than personal life or gain. If José could have chosen not to die, he would have declined that choice, knowing that his death could be used by the Lord in many lives. Today missionary Daniel Reyes, inspired by José's story, leads his church to continue to reach out unrelentingly in the community of Nuevo Paris.

Satan desires to dissuade us from claiming the Lord's promises by tempting us to fear. We are fearful of failure, circumstances, criticism, and even physical harm. We are not alone in such temptation.

The apostle Peter was intimately familiar with personal failure. In the Garden of Gethsemane, he slept while Jesus prayed, and then he cut off the ear of Malchus, the high priest's servant. As the events of the night proceeded, Peter denied his Master three times. His guilt and shame were so severe that they could have ended his ministry. By the precious promises of a forgiving Savior, Peter found His will and embarked on the journey that God had designed for him. Satan lost Peter's battle with the fear of failure. Will he lose yours?

When Satan attempts to silence us with fear, we can confront him with scripture, *"For God hath not given us the spirit of fear; but of power, and of love, and of a sound mind"* (2 Timothy 1:7). Rather than fearing Satan's schemes, we should fear the Lord with so much reverence and allegiance that we would welcome the opportunity to claim His promises and answer His call.

Satan makes every effort to convince us that our circumstances are beyond the power of God's promises to overcome. David faced many circumstances in his life of service to God, but few were more likely to result in failure than his decision to fight Goliath. He trusted his God, and he believed in His cause. It was that simple. The task wasn't easy for David, but victory was sure because of the power of the promises of his God. Do we trust Him in like manner?

Fear of criticism and persecution is one of the most effective weapons in Satan's arsenal. He constantly seeks to eliminate the witness of many Christians with this threat. Jesus was well aware of this tactic of Satan, and addressed it early in the Sermon on the Mount. Matthew records His words, *"Blessed are they which are persecuted for righteousness' sake: for theirs is the kingdom of heaven. Blessed are ye, when men shall revile you, and persecute you, and shall say all manner of evil against you falsely, for my sake. Rejoice, and be exceeding glad: for great is your reward in heaven: for so persecuted they the prophets which were before you"* (Matthew 5:10-12). Such promises provide comfort that can come only from the heart of God. What peace the words of the Savior must have brought to the apostles and so many others who have given their lives for the gospel!

Satan preys upon the prospect of pain and death to use the danger of physical harm as a deterrent to the gospel. He has miserably failed to stop the work of missions with this tool. Throughout history faithful men and women have ignored his schemes, counting the cost of the cause of Christ worthy of their physical sacrifice and confronting danger with the promises of their God. The courage of Stephen cries out from the pages of Scripture, challenging us to full commitment. Not all have been spared physically, but all are partakers of the final victory that awaits. What a joyous moment it will be to stand before Him one day as a faithful missionary. Will you claim this promise of victory? Read 2 Timothy 4:7-8.

The impact of our witness is not limited by time or distance, but is kept alive by the infinite power of our God. The fulfillment of His promises revitalizes the commitment of missionaries each day. He demonstrates the promise of His presence even in the efforts of missionary children to share the gospel.

The tiny community of Tierra Blanca lay two to three hours from the town of Playa Vicente in the state of Veracruz, Mexico. The small band of struggling families that comprised its population spent their days in pursuit of the meager livelihood to which they had been accustomed all their lives. Necessities were hard to obtain, and luxuries were nonexistent. The Lord, however, gave Joe and Belinda Caudle a different perspective of the families of Tierra Blanca. Under the direction of the Holy Spirit, they began to make the lengthy trip each Friday, preparing teaching materials and food to share with these humble people. At first they were met with cautious curiosity. A few families began to accept their friendship.

One family in particular had a large number of children, all trying to survive in a small house that was barely adequate to protect them from the elements. Rosa was five years old when Rachel, the Caudles' young daughter, was called upon to teach her age group each Friday. Rosa was immensely shy and very hesitant to participate in activities, but she slowly began to respond to Rachel's kindness. By the end of the first year of the mission in Tierra Blanca, she had adopted Rachel as her own special friend. Rachel was accustomed to carrying items to give to the children, useful things such as toothbrushes, as well as small toys and delicious treats. Rosa cared for her gifts as if they were treasures.

As the vehicle would arrive in the village, she would hurry out to meet Rachel, eager to begin the lesson and activities. Rachel saturated her time with these children with prayer. Several months passed and she began to speak more specifically to them regarding the plan of salvation. She explained many times the love of Jesus and its availability to all. During these discussions, Rosa, now almost seven years old, was quiet and thoughtful; not openly responding, but listening intently.

One Friday afternoon the Caudles arrived for Bible study only to find that Rosa was not feeling well. She had been experiencing headaches, but had shown no other symptoms. That evening she stayed home. When the Bible study finished, Rachel went to say good-bye to Rosa. She told her that she would be praying that she would feel better soon.

Rachel felt the Spirit prompting her to ask Rosa about giving her heart to Christ. Rosa responded that she would think about it. Rachel gave Rosa one of the coloring books and crayons that she had brought for the children. She silently placed the matter of Rosa's salvation in the Lord's hands, and the Caudles began their journey home to Playa Vicente.

The next morning Brother Caudle awoke to a knock on the door. He went out to see who might be calling, and there, to his shock, was Rosa's father. He had traveled for hours to give the Caudles the heartbreaking news that Rosa had passed away during the night. The doctor suspected a brain aneurysm.

Rachel was stricken with overwhelming emotion, that mixture of deep love and profound loss that only the Lord can comfort. She steadied herself to receive the little bundle that Rosa's father was holding out to her. Inside she found all the little gifts she had given Rosa, everything that had not been a perishable item.

The newest item was the coloring book from the evening before. Rachel gently opened the little book, feeling somehow very close to this beloved child. She slowly turned its pages until she reached one where Rosa had briefly attempted to color. Instantly her eyes were drawn to the corner of the page. There in the characteristic print of a young child were the sweetest words that anyone can speak or pen:

Friday
Rachel, I love you
  Jesus saved me
  Thank you
  Rosa

Reflect, Discuss & Apply

1. Read Hebrews 7:24-25. How does this promise portray the priority that Jesus places upon the salvation of souls?

2. Study 2 Peter 1:3-8. How do these verses relate to the believer's responsibility to share the gospel?

   (verse 3) Call _____

   (verse 4) Promises _____

   (verse 5) Diligence _____

   (verse 8) Fruit _____

3. List the Christlike graces that we are to develop (2 Peter 1:5-7) in order to become servants who fully experience the fulfillment of His promises upon our outreach to souls.

   _____

4. As you remember Rosa and José, whose lives on earth ended at the ages of six and seventeen, discuss why it is so important to reach young people with the gospel.

5. List three examples of God's faithfulness in the life and death of José. Share his testimony with a young person, emphasizing these examples.

   _____

   _____

   _____

6. How can you claim God's promises and overcome your fear of witnessing?

   _____

   _____

3

BY GOD'S FAITHFULNESS

Jesus promised, *"And I, if I be lifted up from the earth, will draw all men unto me"* (John 12:32). God is always faithful in seeking and saving lost souls. He does this through the conviction of the Holy Spirit. The Holy Spirit places a strong desire for spiritual peace in the hearts of lost people whom He is convicting to be saved. A number of testimonies from BMAA mission fields demonstrate God's faithfulness to send the gospel and save sinners.

Brother and Mrs. Paul Heuermann share the story of a young woman in Ghana whose testimony illustrates the Spirit's power. The Heuermanns traveled forty-five miles from their home to the village of Akrofom and arrived at dusk. While waiting for the local pastor to meet them and give directions regarding where to set up equipment to hold the service, the Heuermanns were surrounded by an increasing number of curious children. One little boy in particular caught their attention. He was perhaps two years old and was carrying a bucket almost as big as himself. Brother Heuermann asked him playfully in sign language for his bucket. He handed it over with a big smile, excited to be giving something to an *obroni*, a white man. (African people love to give, in spite of their poverty.)

The little boy's sister soon appeared looking for him, so the Heuermanns returned the bucket, and the two children disappeared in the crowd. The local pastor arrived and, along with the Heuermanns, began to prepare for the service.

Mrs. Heuermann periodically scanned the faces of onlookers hoping to see the two children but to no avail. The service began with music, and then summer missionary David Erickson preached a simple salvation message. The crowd that had gathered was largely composed of children and became increasingly loud and disruptive. However, experienced missionaries know never to give up or assume that the message has not been received. An invitation was given, and out of the darkness came a young woman carrying the little boy who had *loaned* the Heuermanns his bucket. She expressed the desire to be saved, but did not seem to truly comprehend the concept of receiving Christ as personal Savior. She was asked to wait at the front for counseling at the end of the service.

Brother Heuermann, Brother Erickson, and the pastor did not feel led to close the service. After prayer, additional music was presented while adults quieted the children for another message of salvation by Brother Heuermann. The young woman had gradually moved toward the back of the crowd and disappeared from the lighted area. Mrs. Heuermann prayed diligently, fearing that she would leave. The Lord answers prayer. When the second invitation was given, the woman passed the child to his sister and quickly came forward again. She received Christ as her Savior along with several others who followed her to the front.

This young woman stood in the middle of a village street for over two hours in darkness holding a squirming two-year-old boy. She was determined not to leave until she had received assurance of salvation in her heart. Through all the noise and confusion the Holy Spirit had penetrated her heart so profoundly that surrounding circumstances were useless to Satan in his attempt to prevent her salvation.

Although we are not privileged to even know this young woman's name, our God certainly does, and we shall become gloriously acquainted with her in heaven. Praise the Lord for such a blessing! Mrs. Heuermann observes that the African people are deeply hungry for spiritual truth. When the gospel is presented, they are determined to hear it. Are we as determined to share it? Are we willing to be likewise faithful?

As witnesses for Christ we must learn to accept the sinner regardless of present or past conditions. If we expect the sinner to accept Christ despite past experiences, then we must accept the sinner, though not the sin, as a testimony of God's faithfulness to save.

Will dropped out of school in fourth grade to work. This practice is not uncommon in his town of Santa Rosa Copán, Honduras. After all, he was the second oldest in a family of six children. In characteristic human nature Will responded to desperate circumstances with irrational behavior. He would work until he had enough money to buy beer, drink his fill, steal to buy more, and eventually find himself in a brawl with his fellow drunkards. This cycle repeated itself over and over again until it became Will's habitual lifestyle.

In spite of his irresponsibility, Will married at age eighteen and soon became the father of a baby girl. His alcoholic binges did not subside, but rather resulted in increasing violence. Two more children were born, in spite of Will's physical and emotional abuse of his wife. Will's drinking meant there was never enough money for food, clothing, or medical care.

Will drifted from day to day becoming more and more complacent. Seemingly, nothing could jolt him to face reality. Then news arrived that his mother-in-law had been murdered. For the first time Will faced his own mortality and was paralyzed with fear about his spiritual condition. He and his wife went to visit the neighbors, Brother and Mrs. Tom Jopling. Sitting in the tabernacle one evening Will and his wife gave their hearts to Jesus. Their home experienced radical changes that could only have come from Jesus.

The rest of the story is a victorious journey of growth in grace. Will has an insatiable hunger for God's Word and for the fellowship of his brothers and sisters in Christ. He has been transformed into a loving husband and father to his wife and four children. He has witnessed to members of his extended family and has enjoyed the blessing of seeing his sister and brother saved, as well as others to whom he has witnessed. He sought out family members to help him improve his reading skills so that he could better understand the Bible. He teaches Sunday School, gives devotionals, and is regarded by the youth of his neighborhood as someone from whom they can seek trustworthy spiritual counsel. Will has made known his call to the ministry. At age twenty-four he is a shining example of God's faithfulness.

The story of Hong Suk Koh shows that we serve a God Who has the power to raise up the son of poor South Korean Shaman Buddhist farmers, bring him at the age of thirty to the United States, lead him to a Bible study, convict him to be saved, teach him the Word, and send him to the Mojave Desert where God had a ministry for him. Our omniscient God knew that a community of Koreans and Korean-Americans would develop in the High Desert of California. He knew that they would have grave spiritual needs complicated by differences in culture and language and that they would need a servant to be called into their community who would understand by experience their spiritual plight.

God knew that by the power of His Holy Spirit Hong Suk Koh would be willing to surrender to His will and that he would be humble enough to minister to these people, whom he would love dearly. In Brother Koh's words, he went to the Koreans of the Mojave Desert to "make myself a testimony." Are we guilty of neglecting to encourage, support, and pray for servants such as Brother and Mrs. Koh, who sacrifice their lives in carrying the gospel to people to whom the Lord has specially equipped them to minister?

Many times it is difficult for us to understand the mysterious plan of the Lord for bringing souls to Christ. We are to simply obey, watch in faith, and trust as He works. Sometimes we must watch converts fall into temptation and suffer the chastisement required to bring them back into the will of God. Such was the case of Jose, who was saved in the BMAA church in San Pedro Sula, Honduras. His story was shared by Brother and Mrs. David Beirne.

Soon after his conversion José began to try to mix faith on Sunday with sin during the week. His testimony began to suffer. The church began to pray earnestly for his spiritual restoration, and soon he responded to the conviction in his heart. He shed many tears as he confessed before the church asking for forgiveness and prayer.

José committed himself to witness to his marijuana-smoking pals. During one particular series of services, he rejoiced as seven of them accepted Christ as Savior. From a human perspective it seemed that Jose was being prepared for a great ministry.

The Lord, however, in His divine will was preparing to use José in a different way. Unexpectedly, he became very sick. The doctors diagnosed meningitis and hospitalized him for a month. It appeared as if his treatment was going well, and his friends became excited about the witness he would be able to give once he was healed. Then his condition reversed, and his body deteriorated while many agonized over why he would be allowed to die. At his funeral service just six weeks later, many youth of the community heard the gospel for the first time. One more also heard — José's grandmother. Though very steeped in the traditions of her professed religion, she began to attend church services following the funeral. The seed of the gospel had been planted, and through the preached Word the Holy Spirit brought the Word to life in her heart. One night during an invitation she cried out, "I want to accept Christ tonight." What a victory in death! God can turn what often appears to be certain tragedy into blessing. In His faithfulness, He uses many experiences to draw men and women unto His Son.

In His faithfulness, God also uses different forms of ministry to reach people. The summer before my family moved to Uruguay as missionaries, my father made a trip to Brazil along with several pastors and missions directors. Upon his arrival back at home in Texas, my mother and I were eager to hear about all that he had seen and experienced. I vividly recall my daddy describing the mission work he had visited in Brazil. He was particularly touched by the work he observed in the towns of Campinas, which I later visited, and Corinto. The testimony of the longtime pastor of the Vila Maciel church in Corinto is a testament to the unwavering faithfulness of God.

Timoteo Carneiro began his young adulthood as a construction worker on the railroad which was built to link the port of Santos, Brazil, to the city of Santa Cruz, Bolivia. His training as an engineer took him to the railroad shops in the town of Corinto. For the next thirty years he drove the locomotives of the Brazilian rail system, a vital mode of transportation in that era.

Under the leadership of Pastor Josias C. Castro the BMAA church in Corinto launched an outreach to the railroad employees who had migrated to the city. A fellow engineer who had accepted Christ witnessed to Timoteo. He, too, received Jesus into his heart and became a traveling witness up and down the rails of the state of Minas Gerais, unashamedly sharing the gospel message that Jesus saves souls and transforms lives.

Using his delightful sense of humor, Timoteo altered the lyrics of a popular chorus, "With Christ in the vessel, we can laugh at the storm." Brother Timoteo's version became the anthem of his locomotive, "With Christ in the locomotive, everything's all right."

The Lord spared Brother Timoteo in two separate serious accidents because He had work for him to do. He served first as a deacon and helped build the sanctuary of the Vila Maciel church. He surrendered to the call of the ministry, eventually becoming the pastor of his home church until his death. He traveled and preached, faithfully defending the Word. He passed the importance of missions on to his children. Are we as faithful in training the generation that will follow us?

Reflect, Discuss & Apply

1. Write your testimony of salvation, specifically including the ways in which God's faithfulness brought the gospel to you.
2. Ask the Lord to lead you in sharing your testimony with someone who is unsaved and with someone who simply needs an encouraging reminder of God's faithfulness.
3. How can you be faithful to encourage missionaries? Read their articles and newsletters, e-mail or write them, attend services when they give presentations. What can you add to this list?
4. From articles written by missionaries find at least two examples of God's faithfulness on a mission field. Share these testimonies.
5. Read Lamentations 3:23, 1 Thessalonians 5:24, and 2 Thessalonians 3:3. What are the promises of these passages which you can claim daily in your personal witnessing and in your prayers for missionaries?

4

BY GOD'S POWER

Missionary work led by the Holy Spirit will enjoy the Lord's blessings and the salvation of souls. God's message to mankind has always been conveyed by the Holy Spirit. Peter declared that the message is to go forth not by the will or design of man but by the direction of the Holy Spirit. This was true in Old Testament times, in the early church of the New Testament, and still today. In 2 Peter 1:21, Peter reminds us that, *"prophecy came not in old time by the will of man: but holy men of God spake as they were moved by the Holy Ghost."*

There is no substitute for the work of the Holy Spirit in missionary outreach. Believers are called by the Holy Spirit to share Jesus Christ; the Word of God is conveyed by the Holy Spirit to hearts that He has prepared; the Holy Spirit calls souls to repentance. Therefore, we must seek the presence and power of the Holy Spirit in our lives if we aspire to be His instrument in the work of missions.

Missionaries share many testimonies of the power of God in their ministries. The saving grace of the Lord knows no boundaries. It is impossible for someone to become so wretched a sinner that the love of God is out of reach. No case is too hopeless, no soul is too lost, that His life-changing love cannot transform. The only persons who are denied the hope of salvation are those who reject Christ forever. We are to go forth boldly in His mighty power and send others where we cannot go to carry the message of salvation.

Satan has managed to remove boldness from the arsenal of many believers. One tactic he has used is to convince society that *religion* is a totally private matter, never to be discussed in public. Many believers capitulate to this pressure to silence their witness. He has created the image that believers should be weak, quiet, retreating souls who allow their faith to show only within the walls of the church. Another tactic Satan uses is his attempt to convince many believers that the only way they can have Christian influence is to engage in the same lifestyles, interests, and behavior of those whom they wish to win to Christ.

Satan's next step down this path of thinking is to convince believers to become ashamed before our acquaintances of our belief in the need for salvation. What a sad victory to give Satan. This spiritual condition dilutes our witness and poisons our lives.

The power of Jesus Christ can overcome Satan and make us the missionaries He intends us to be. When we face the judgment of Christ, what we have done to win souls to Him will be our only focus. Christ offers a sobering challenge. Either we are His servants, or we are not. Our decision has eternal consequences for both ourselves and the lost world. Missions is truly the essence of eternity.

Missionary Tom Jopling shares such a case in the account of the salvation of a father in Honduras. Upon their arrival in Honduras the Jopling family began their mission outreach on an individual basis, first as good neighbors. Brother Jopling was able to provide assistance such as transportation to a funeral for the family living next door. Later, a child in the same family needed blood for surgery, and Brother Jopling donated the blood. The Joplings initiated front-porch Bible studies for the many children in their neighborhood. To their delight many began to attend accompanied by their mothers, who enjoyed activities such as coloring as much as their children. Among these ladies was Uvy, the mother of the family to whom Brother Jopling had ministered on the two previous occasions. Eventually Uvy's interest in the message of Christ began to grow. Soon she requested that Brother and Mrs. Jopling visit in her home to share Jesus with her family. She wanted her husband to hear the gospel. The conviction of the Holy Spirit was evident and powerful as the Joplings shared the gospel message with the entire family, including a son from the father's previous marriage. When Brother Jopling finished witnessing to this family, the father chose to speak for them all and informed Brother Jopling that none of them would accept Christ. With burdened hearts the Joplings returned home to commit this family to the Lord in daily prayer. Uvy and her children, Eddie, age thirteen, Olbán, age twelve, and Margarita, age five, continued to attend services. Eddie moved to the larger city of San Pedro to work. Mrs. Jopling was able to lead Olbán to Christ following a church service. Soon afterward, Uvy found the courage to accept Christ as her Savior. When the entire family moved to San Pedro, Brother Jopling asked permission for Olbán to live with the Jopling family to go to school. Eddie accepted Christ in San Pedro and returned home to be baptized in the mission. On the evening of Easter of that same year he drowned. Praise the Lord that the gospel had reached him! Once again, Brother Jopling was able to minister in a time of great need. As he assisted with Eddie's funeral service, the father was by his side. One week later this man confided to Brother Jopling that God had to take his son to soften his heart, but that he was now ready to receive Christ. God continues to work in the lives of this family. The Holy Spirit can empower our efforts to share the gospel when we are helpless to do so!

While sharing the message of God's power to save with the lost, we sometimes encounter people who feel that they are so sinful that God could never rescue them from their plight. We must rely on the Holy Spirit for words of wisdom to convince them otherwise.

One of Satan's strongholds in Africa has been witchcraft. Amos was raised in the environment this lifestyle creates. His home was devoted to the worship of Satan and the evil practices this religion involves. As a child he had been educated in the sacrifice of animals and humans to Satan and had eaten the brew made from organs of those sacrificed. He had received supernatural power from Satan to read the minds of other people. He knew beyond a shadow of doubt that his soul belonged to Satan and that his eternal destiny would be hell.

One morning Amos awoke gravely ill. His condition was so serious that he knew he was dying. He began to cry out to his *friends* that he did not want to die. They, of course, could not help him.

God uses people and circumstances in ways that are a mystery to us. Amos' friends told him that the *Christians* could tell him how he could avoid dying. He sought them out immediately, and they shared the message of salvation through the sacrificial blood of Jesus. The power of the Holy Spirit conveyed the message to Amos' aching heart, and he cried out in faith, believing and trusting Jesus as his personal Savior. That night he slept for the first time he could remember without his spirit struggling in evil out-of-the-body experiences. He had found peace of mind knowing that he was beyond Satan's reach and that in life or in death he would be safe in the arms of Jesus. What a powerful God we serve!

Vasiliy was saved at the age of twenty-nine under the ministry of missionary Boris Volshonok. The road to his conversion required the power of God to be manifested in a persistent witness. Born the youngest of four boys, he had naturally looked up to his oldest brother. This state of affairs began to change, however, when his oldest brother was invited to attend services in the local Baptist church and decided to go.

Before long, Vasiliy's brother began to speak of an experience called salvation which required one to admit being a sinner and become born again. Vasiliy felt these words were empty; his mind could not fathom such a belief. He felt his brother had become mentally disturbed. Vasiliy had heard about God and the Bible all his life, but his only interest had stemmed from being told that the Bible reveals the end of the world. Bibles were almost impossible to obtain in Belarus during Vasiliy's childhood.

One day Vasiliy received a copy of the Gospel of John. Though he read it, he dismissed it as mere historical information. The following year Vasiliy finally acquired a New Testament. He read as far as the book of Acts, but finding the reading boring he stored the book on a shelf. Three years passed before he slowly began to open its pages again. His brother prayed for opportunities to witness to Vasiliy, and through the power of the Holy Spirit conviction began to have its impact. Vasiliy responded by falling deeper and deeper into sin, eventually losing his marriage because of his daily habits.

Alone and depressed Vasiliy finally opened his mind to the possibility of God's love and forgiveness. He saw the emptiness of his soul and the filthiness of sin in his heart. He sat down to watch the movie *Jesus*, a gift from his brother's church. That very evening he knelt and asked Jesus to come into his heart, forgive his sin, and give him a brand new life. The Lord restored his marriage and set his feet upon a new path. Vasiliy ponders the road he might have traveled if no one had sent missionaries to his country, if those whom the Lord called had refused to go, and if his brother had resisted the gospel or simply not cared about his soul. Vasiliy's story challenges us to bear the precious gospel of Christ!

We should pray for sensitivity to the Holy Spirit's direction that He could prompt us when we encounter someone who is open to the gospel. Missionary Darlene Carey travels a great deal in the Philippines assisting missions, churches, youth, and evangelistic teams in outreach ministries. Open-air services have proven very effective in reaching those who might not choose to attend a formal service in a church building. These services often include a puppet show, a concert by singing groups, and then the preaching of the Word. Such was the plan of a team of workers who traveled to the town of E. B. Magalona. They set up their equipment in the public plaza and proceeded through the normal activities, giving an invitation at the conclusion of the gospel message. Several raised their hands indicating interest in salvation. Counselors fanned out into the crowd throughout the plaza to respond to those who had raised their hands. One counselor sat down with two high school students, read scriptures to them, and explained the plan of salvation. Both of the young people prayed for salvation, and the counselor continued by giving them scriptures for study and instructing them on how to begin to grow in their faith. She invited them to attend Sunday school and church services at the BMA church in E. B. Magalona.

As the conversation ended, the counselor heard the voice of a younger child behind her who was asking for directions to the church. His name was Rolando, and he was in the sixth grade. To her joy the counselor discovered that Rolando had been listening to the conversation with the teenagers and had prayed along with them for salvation.

On the first Sunday following this experience Rolando attended services alone. Alert to the possibility of meeting his family Darlene and others offered him a ride home. They met his mother and led her to Christ. The family is now faithful in service and have opened their home for weekly Bible studies for evangelistic outreach to friends and neighbors. Their story reminds us that God is in control when we witness, and that He knows whose heart may be yearning for truth. Someone may literally be listening "over our shoulder," as Darlene so aptly observed.

Reflect, Discuss & Apply

1. Read Matthew 28:18. How can you begin to experience God's boldness and power in witnessing?

2. Read Romans 1:16. What can you do to resist the temptation of Satan to be ashamed of the gospel and the cause of missions?

3. Reflect upon occasions in which you have witnessed the power of God in the salvation of souls. Share these testimonies of spiritual victory.

4. Ask the Lord to lay upon your heart the name of a sister in Christ who is burdened for a lost family member or friend. Write Ephesians 6:10 on a note card and give it to that person.

5. Read Ephesians 1:17-23. How can you enlarge your vision of serving each day in His power?

5

BY GOD'S GRACE AND MERCY

How difficult it is to convey to the lost that salvation comes as a gift by the grace and mercy of the Savior. In a world which champions personal effort as the means to gain everything and where religions have taught for millenniums that spiritual redemption is to be earned by good works, how can we convince people of the true plan of salvation? The answer lies in our lives. We must show by our daily walk that the love of Christ is free to everyone. Remember that Jesus' love was unshakable and unchangeable even when He hung on the cross. Lost people must see all of Christ's love, mercy, grace, and forgiveness in us.

Lost souls in distant regions may never meet us personally. But our prayers, sacrificial giving, and missions support can enable them to hear the true plan of salvation and offer a testimony before them. We must examine ourselves regularly to determine if our lives are sending the gospel message to the world.

Many cultures are saturated with religious teachings that are completely incompatible with the doctrine of a merciful God. It is very difficult for people who are exposed to such beliefs to abandon that indoctrination and accept the mercy of God. Religious systems which teach that one must earn redemption breed guilt and fear. Yet many missionaries must witness to people in such a spiritual condition.

These missionaries exemplify how we can show the grace and mercy of the Lord through daily living. Circumstances do not deter them. They do whatever it takes for however long it takes to demonstrate the grace and mercy of Christ to individuals for whom they are burdened.

The Collin Jones family shares a testimony from the field of Honduras of the victory that results in lives from such a steadfast witness. When Ginger Jones first met Gloria, Gloria was unwilling to attend Bible study groups. She was a very sweet, kind mother of five children but extremely shy. She had no friends and avoided relating to people. Ginger began to visit her for a few minutes once or twice each week. A friendship began to develop. Though Gloria would not reciprocate the visits, she did begin to greet Ginger with a smile, and the time spent together began to slowly increase. Ginger began to witness to Gloria during the visits. Gloria would ask questions and listen intently, but she could not find the courage to give her life to Christ.

Ginger noticed a distinct sadness and continual physical exhaustion in Gloria. She decided to show her the love of God through personal service. Ginger began to pick up the family laundry every Monday morning. As Mrs. Jones washed the clothes, hung them out to dry, and folded them, she saturated each family member with prayer. She asked the Lord to show her ways to demonstrate His grace to Gloria.

This simple selfless act, repeated each week, convinced Gloria that the missionaries truly cared for her, and she attended her first Bible study. However, Satan always has a plan. Gloria began to use her baby as an excuse to avoid the adult study. Ginger and others decided to help with the baby at the Bible study to draw Gloria into the group.

Behind every hurting face there is usually a story of pain and hurt. Gloria was no exception. She had experienced rejection by her parents as a child and abuse at the hands of various relatives who had taken her into their home. She had never enjoyed a stable, loving home and feared that her husband, who had taken her for his wife when she was fourteen years old, would abandon her also.

One Sunday Gloria's husband told the missionaries that she had developed a severe toothache. Mrs. Jones promptly made an appointment for Gloria with her personal dentist. Upon arriving to carry Gloria to the dentist, the missionaries found her very weak and sick. A doctor from the mission took care of her, and a family in the mission provided food.

Gloria had reached her moment of decision. In her weakened physical condition, her heart cried out for help. She shared her deep concern for one of her daughters. Ginger counseled her that trusting God is the answer to every problem we face. She was able to use the illustration of Gloria's love and concern for her daughter as an example of God's love and concern for her. Gloria humbly acknowledged her need for the Savior. She prayed and accepted Christ that very night.

The following Sunday, Gloria once again attended Bible study, this time participating with newfound joy. Following her conversion, Gloria's oldest son, Mario, was also saved. Together they studied Bible lessons provided by the missionaries and witnessed to Gloria's oldest daughter, who was saved and now studies with them.

All these experiences have helped Gloria understand God's love, grace, and mercy. The mentoring she is receiving from her new brothers and sisters in Christ is teaching her the true meaning of friendship. She is learning to study God's Word and beginning to recognize that He has a special plan for her life. She is growing in awareness that He has equipped her for service by blessing her with abilities, talents, and spiritual gifts. She is learning that she is a very important and unique part of a very special group, her church, and that she can make a real difference in the lives of others. She is learning that her church needs her and that it suffers without her.

None of the life-changing events that Gloria has experienced could have occurred without the grace and mercy of the Lord in sending missionaries to carry the gospel. These men and women have committed themselves to living out His grace and mercy in others' lives. Is there joy in doing this? Mrs. Jones answers with unwavering certainty, "I am so thankful that God sent my family to Honduras to teach Gloria and others like her what the love of God is. It is exciting to watch them come alive through salvation and discover God's plan for their lives. I never thought as a young lady that God would use me to touch the lives of people of another language and culture. I am thankful that God has sent me to Honduras and used me and my family to bring others to Christ and help them develop as Christians." Don't allow Satan to deny you the joy of serving in the Lord's great army of missionaries. He has a place for you to serve. He's waiting for you to be a willing instrument of His marvelous grace and infinite mercy.

What a challenge we face in our world to show the mercy of Christ. While the world thinks in terms of justice, we are called upon to be instruments of mercy. We are to saturate our lives with the mercy of Christ until we become vessels which pour out His mercy into the lives of everyone around us. Our flesh resists such a lifestyle. Therefore, our only recourse is to deny the flesh, embrace the mind of Christ, and live in the Spirit. God, in His mercy, will honor our sincere commitment to do this. Jesus warned us in Mark 14:38, *"The spirit truly is ready, but the flesh is weak."*

One of the most effective motivations to show the mercy of the Lord to the lost is to remind ourselves where we would be without mercy. Without mercy we would be totally and eternally lost. This fact should humble us, bring us to our knees in repentance of halfhearted service, and remove any trace of self-righteousness and arrogance from our daily walk.

Consider how long-suffering God's mercy has been. God has a long history of dealing with humanity in mercy. In Noah's day, men and women were given abundant opportunity to repent before judgment rained upon them. The Old Testament is replete with examples of God's mercy extended to Israel. He has showered mercy upon His church and modern society. We are also given ample examples of His judgment. Knowing that He wishes to use us to show mercy to the lost and bring them to repentance, we must set about this task, trusting His instruction and strength.

The Lord's patient mercy to lost souls compels us to never give up on those to whom He has called us to witness. Veteran missionaries Paul and Mickey Robinson have witnessed such experiences throughout their ministry. One such testimony originates in a humble Houston home. A family of unbelievers allowed a small group to gather and discuss the gospel message. The husband arrived late, was scantily dressed, and sat down on the floor by a wall. His demeanor demonstrated that he was not interested in the proceedings. The next week the man became increasingly uncomfortable, only allowing the believers to return to avoid hurt feelings. By the third week, he had moved without notifying the missionaries. Since the man was an alcoholic, the prospect of reaching him seemed very bleak. No one, however, is beyond the reach of the mercy of God.

Several months passed with no word from this family. Then one Sunday the two daughters appeared in a worship service at the Center of Life. The Holy Spirit began to convict their hearts, and they each received Christ. They became very active in the church and also in an action center.

New Year's Eve arrived, and the parents, father and mother together, attended the watch night service at the church. Soon the father made a profession of faith, but the mother remained skeptical of his decision. She felt he was simply attempting to escape legal problems and would soon revert to his old ways. When she saw his genuine change, she too accepted Christ as her Savior. The father, who had been illiterate, learned how to read from the Bible. He studied faithfully, eventually becoming an action center leader. When the Bible institute was opened, he enrolled. He subsequently answered God's call to the ministry.

The work of the Holy Spirit in the life of Brother Oscar and Sister Eligia Alfaro continues today as they minister in the city of Abilene, Texas. Both of their daughters also serve the Lord faithfully.

Brother John Elliott relates many testimonies of the grace of God demonstrated in lives throughout the history of BMA mission work in Brazil. One such testimony reveals the mercy of the Lord in delivering the lost from superstition to faith.

In 1930, Doña Otacilia moved from the state of Bahía to the city of Pirapora. She was devoutly religious and dreamed of traveling to the shrine of Bom Jesus da Lapa (Good Jesus of Lapa) to pay a vow to the saint. Such a trip would require a riverboat ride to the town of Lapa. Otacilia's sister Esther lived in a region to the north and had trusted Christ as Savior. When she heard of Otacilia's plan to travel to the shrine at Lapa, she determined that she would meet her there to witness to her about Jesus.

Accompanied by a worker from the mission, Esther did exactly as she planned, intercepting Otacilia in Lapa before she could set out for the cave where the shrine was located. Esther shared with her sister the good news of peace and hope in the living Jesus. Otacilia's heart was immediately moved, and she accepted Christ.

Upon returning to her home in Pirapora, Otacilia

joined the Baptist church. When the need for a church building became critical, she joined with other women to carry water in buckets to mix mud for mortar.

At the age of eighty-nine years Doña Otacilia, as she was respectfully and fondly called, went home to be with the Lord. She left a lifetime of service to the Lord and a legacy of a faithful witness to the saving grace and mercy of her God.

We are not called to haul water in buckets, but we are called to find our place of service and commit to the task. Doña Otacilia was such an example of commitment!

Reflect, Discuss & Apply

1. Define the words *grace* and *mercy*. How can we embrace and share Christ's perspectives toward the lost?

2. Examine your attitude toward lost people. How can you demonstrate the grace and mercy of Christ? Ask the Lord to lay upon your heart someone such as Gloria who needs Jesus. How can you minister His grace and mercy to that person?

3. Think about the mercy shown by the Lord to the apostle Paul. Commit to pray for persons who are well-known enemies of the gospel.

4. Read Ephesians 2:5-10. Having been humbled by the knowledge that eternal life is a gift, what are some actions you can take to send out the message that this same gift is available to all?

5. Read Romans 10:9-13. What are the promises flowing from the grace and mercy of God which can motivate us to pursue the salvation of souls?

6

BY GOD'S PROTECTION

Jesus promises to walk with us throughout our journey as His missionaries in Matthew 28:20, *"Lo, I am with you alway, even unto the end of the world."*

Throughout history God's servants have faced many adversities in carrying the gospel to dangerous points around the world. Many have braved border crossings trusting the Lord to conceal the treasure of God's Word hidden in car trunks. Others have boldly proclaimed the gospel in public places while jeering mobs threatened their lives. The New Testament offers testimonies of early church saints who counted the cost of spreading the gospel and found it worthy of their sacrifice.

The Lord has promised to protect His message as it is spread throughout the world to the lost. He has assured us that His Word *"endureth for ever ... the word which by the gospel is preached unto you"* (1 Peter 1:25). The psalmist David declared that *"his truth endureth to all generations"* (Psalm 100:5). Mark records Jesus preaching, *"Heaven and earth shall pass away: but my words shall not pass away"* (Mark 13:31).

Hearing stories of God's supernatural protection over His servants inspires and challenges Christians. We are also touched when we hear testimonies of those whom the Lord chose to call to heaven while they were engaged in proclaiming the gospel.

Humans are tempted to claim God's promise of His unfailing presence as a guarantee of immunity from bodily harm or death. This perception is, of course, not the case. God views our physical life and welfare from the perspective of His divine will. He promises to protect our physical bodies within the context of carrying out His will. He often does heal from illness and protect from injury and death. His protection enables us to carry out His plans in the pursuit of lost souls. Therefore, every breath we take is a gift from Him intended to be used in the ministry He has given. Those who live boldly for the Lord, appearing to ignore physical danger and adversity, have learned from experience to make each day count for Christ. We can trust Him to spare our life as long as He has work for us to do. No force of evil can harm us unless the Lord permits it in His will. He can sometimes use evil to bring about good in our own lives or the lives of others.

Satan seeks to deceive us into thinking that if our witnessing shows no visible results it is wasted. Many testimonies challenge this falsehood. One is the story of Rolando, a vibrant Honduran Christian who has surrendered his life to winning his people to Christ. Rolando first heard about Jesus at the age of six. Rolando drifted away from church attendance during elementary school and began to participate in sinful activities. He made many wrong choices and got involved with ungodly friends. But the seed that had been planted in his young heart was alive and well. After many years Rolando arrived at a moment of decision in which he knew he must come to Christ or destroy himself.

Through the power of the Holy Spirit, Rolando made the right decision in an evangelistic service under the ministry of Brother and Mrs. Bill Gibson in the Tabernacle Baptist Church in Sula, Honduras. He has subsequently won his mother to the Lord, attended Bible institute, and is now teaching the Bible to children. Those who commit themselves to the ministry will face trials. Rolando has developed a condition believed to be epilepsy. However, he knows that his victory is in Jesus. He is committed to the salvation of souls in Honduras.

Rolando's example challenges us to witness in spite of personal suffering. Such a commitment will allow our witness to bear fruit long after our ministry in a certain location has passed.

Many missionaries face the barrier of idol worship in their efforts to share the light of truth. American Christians should examine our society, identify the idols that prevail, and ensure that we do not fall into idolatry of our own. We should also be thankful for the blessing of not living in the darkness of satanic worship. Oh, how our missionaries need for us to be their prayer warriors in this realm. Brother John Lindsey vividly shares one such encounter, "It looked to me like a lump of clay some child may have tried to form into an animal. It wasn't very impressive. A black, gummy substance, recognizable as dried blood, was at its base, and scattered around it were singed and fire-blackened feathers." He had expected the community idol to be more distinguished, perhaps covered with gold. The realization struck him that it is not the idol itself that the desperately deceived people worship, but rather the supernatural power it represents. They fear the destructive activity of the demonic evil spirits that they observe every day of their lives. They are compelled by this paralyzing fear to bow down and worship hell itself.

Missionaries must first convince people who are living in such darkness that religion is not the answer to their spiritual needs. If religion were the key to entering heaven, then at least eighty percent of the population of Ghana, and the vast majority of Africans, would be destined to go there because they are extremely religious. They believe intensely in the spiritual realm and fervently follow the priests of their religion.

Even more challenging for the missionary is the sa-

hardened hearts. When the father was stabbed by an attacker in the street, Pastor and Mrs. Rioja spent many hours ministering to the family with food and care.

One day Mrs. Rioja arrived at the church expecting it to be empty. She found Wincie sitting quietly alone. She led her to Christ in that quiet moment. When the younger sister became very sick, Jacklyn's mother finally spoke to Mrs. Rioja for the first time, acknowledging her sincere concern and thanking her for all that had been done for her family.

Jacklyn continues to be an outspoken witness for Christ, having won many of her peers to the Lord. She and Wincie continue to grow in Christ. Jacklyn desires to attend the BMA Bible College. Surely the Lord has spared her life in order that she may fulfill His great plans for her in the future. She has been prepared through personal trials to minister and carry the gospel to many whose hurt she will deeply understand. God's protection over His message and the messengers extends also to all who will receive it.

People who need to hear the gospel are all around us. The Lord wants to use us to share His message with total strangers and our closest loved ones. Are we guilty of overlooking those who need our witness?

Public buses are a common mode of transportation in the towns of Costa Rica. These public buses themselves contain a mission field. Gratefully this truth was not lost upon one dedicated believer from the mission in Desamparados. She boarded a bus and sat down by a lady and proceeded to witness about Christ. The conversation was very simple and lasted only a few minutes. But the impact was profound. Out of curiosity Laura Rojas, the lady to whom the believer had witnessed, appeared on a Thursday night in the church to which she had been invited to Bible study. As events unfolded, she began to share the events of her past.

Unfortunately, her story is all too typical of her generation of Latin American young people. She had been a young university student in the seventies when the pressure was incredibly intense to join in the popular Marxist-Socialist political activism. She committed herself to this cause with great fervor, joining the revolutionary movements throughout Central America, and actually fighting in the civil war in Nicaragua. She spent fourteen years there, where she married. Upon the death of her husband in the military conflict, she became disillusioned with political and social movements and turned her attention to a search that penetrated her soul even more deeply. She longed for spiritual peace. For nine years she faithfully served in Jehovah's Witnesses, but did not find the fulfillment she was seeking.

In her hour of confusion the Lord sent the believer from the Baptist mission in Desamparados to take her seat beside Laura on the bus. The process of witnessing to Laura was to prove more difficult than it first seemed, however. Laura was well armed with questions, doubts, false doctrines, and plenty of ill-conceived rationales to support them. Her arguments challenged those witnessing to her to truly depend on the Lord for the words that would penetrate her heart. To their surprise she returned again and again to hear more of the Word. Finally her heart was softened, and she cried for joy as she received Christ into her heart. Shortly afterward her daughter followed her example and was saved. God had protected Laura through years of drifting in godless movements to bring her eventually to Christ.

Reflect, Discuss & Apply

1. Do you know someone who has drifted away from church attendance and is experimenting in a worldly lifestyle? Ask the Lord to give you an opportunity to lovingly share Rolando's testimony with that person.
2. Consider the protection God provided for Noah, Moses, David, Daniel, Shadrach, Meshach, and Abednego. Review the experiences of Paul, Silas, Peter, and all those who have faithfully passed the gospel down through the centuries. Though many eventually gave their lives for the gospel, they ministered under the safety of God until their calling was completed. Make them your heroes; draw strength from their example daily.
3. While reading articles or stories written by missionaries, watch for a specific testimony of God's protection in carrying the gospel. Share the story with someone whom Satan is attacking in the effort to serve Him.
4. Note that in the sequence of scripture, Psalm 90:17 immediately precedes the beautiful promises of protection in Psalm 91. In verse seventeen, the psalmist asks God to ordain our acts of service. Offer this prayer daily, and go forward trusting in His will.

7

BY OUR SURRENDER

It is interesting that in the Gospel of Mark two verses separate the writer's account of Jesus' calling sinners in Galilee to repentance and His calling Galileans to be missionaries. Mark quotes Jesus, *"The time is fulfilled, and the kingdom of God is at hand: repent ye, and believe the gospel"* (Mark 1:15). Later, as He walked by the sea of Galilee, He called to Simon and Andrew, *"Come ye after me, and I will make you to become fishers of men"* (Mark 1:17). He issued the call so simply and concisely yet so urgently.

Surrendering to the will of the Lord honors our Savior's purpose for saving us. He calls each of us as witnesses, missionaries to a lost world. Mission work was so critical to Jesus that He commanded his disciples to pray for willing workers, *"The harvest truly is plenteous, but the labourers are few; pray ye therefore the Lord of the harvest, that he will send forth labourers into his harvest"* (Matthew 9:37-38). In John 4:35, Jesus issued the command, *"Lift up your eyes, and look on the fields; for they are white already to harvest."* Luke was inspired to record the same instructions from Jesus in Luke 10:2.

God calls every believer to carry out His specific plan. He knew us before we were conceived, and He had a specific plan for us. God revealed to Jeremiah, *"Before I formed thee in the belly I knew thee; and before thou camest forth out of the womb I sanctified thee, and I ordained thee a prophet unto the nations"* (Jeremiah 1:5). You can also read the examples given in Isaiah 44:2

and Isaiah 49:1. Every believer should seek the guidance of the Holy Spirit to find that place of service and surrender to it. None of us is exempt from this responsibility.

We surrender ourselves to many things in life. We cherish the pursuits to which we surrender our time, effort, and resources. Some people surrender to a job or career. Some pursue material wealth or fame. Others commit for service to country or humanity. Some choose to promote ideologies. All of these pursuits have both positive and negative aspects. They all, however, are best accomplished and correctly prioritized when they are preceded by the surrender of our entire being to Christ and His perfect will. He desires to direct the path that our lives will take. The path He chooses for each of us leads to joy, peace, and the spiritual happiness He wants us to experience.

When God calls a person to a particular service, He is fully capable of placing a deep and true desire in that soul for devotion to that area of service. Many who have served in places or positions that would seem miserable on a human level can testify to that truth. Remarkably, these people offer assurance that they find their work, although often difficult, to be ultimately rewarding and fulfilling. The fruits of the Spirit are often most evident in the lives of those who are committed to ministry.

The first and most important qualification for serving as a missionary for our Savior is an intimate relationship with Him. We must live in His Word and walk daily by His precepts. Otherwise the world's priorities and temptations will constantly distract us. Our mission is completely incompatible with worldly ambition. Worldly ambitions are always self-centered and self-serving. They target the carnal ambition of material pursuit or social gain. Our mission targets the spiritual being and the destiny of the eternal soul. Worldly ambitions stress personal pleasure and gratification as a daily reward for effort. Our mission reaps a pure joy of the heart and peace of the soul that passes all understanding. When adversity strikes the pursuit of worldly ambitions, fear immobilizes the best-laid plans. When adversity strikes our mission, our Lord demonstrates His might and power, increasing our faith. Success in worldly ambitions is too often measured by the yardstick of competition. Success in our mission is measured by our degree of obedience to our Lord.

The second qualification for serving as missionaries is the willingness to follow the guidance of the Holy Spirit. We cannot clearly hear His voice unless we are fully surrendered to a life of prayer and immersed daily in His Word. Witnesses miss many opportunities because we are not attuned to the Spirit's prompting when we encounter someone who is lost.

In addition, we must realize that missions is God's plan. He places each of His servants where He chooses. He calls us to the field where He wants us to share the gospel. If we trust Him, He will provide opportunities for us to witness. The Holy Spirit always accompanies our obedience; He convicts hearts with the truth. The harvest of souls rests in the hands of the Lord.

In order to be fit messengers of the love of Christ to a world of lost sinners, we must be transformed by His love and through His blood. We must be conformed to His image by falling in love with Him so completely that we surrender to His lordship. We must love His will so much that we seek to know it above all else. We must love His Word so much that we seek its feeding continually. We must love His presence so much that we seek a perpetual attitude of prayer. We must love His power so much that we seek the constant guidance of the Holy Spirit. We must love His precepts so much that we yearn to obey His commandments. We must love His creation so much that we value the salvation of souls above our own lives.

Only when we have allowed Him to cultivate this character will we be prepared to serve. It is remarkable that in His Sermon on the Mount, Jesus moved immediately from the Beatitudes to a declaration of the Great Commission's mandate. *"Ye are the salt of the earth: but if the salt have lost his savour, wherewith shall it be salted? It is thenceforth good for nothing, but to be cast out, and to be trodden under foot of men. Ye are the light of the world. A city that is set on an hill cannot be hid. Neither do men light a candle, and put it under a bushel, but on a candlestick; and it giveth light unto all that are in the house. Let your light so shine before men, that they may see your good works, and glorify your Father which is in heaven"* (Matthew 5:13-16).

I vividly recall an experience when I was twelve that crystallized the concept of Jesus as the Light of our lives, enabling us to be His light to the world. My parents and I were traveling on a ship to become BMAA missionaries in Uruguay. During the three-week voyage the anticipation of our arrival in Montevideo grew with each passing day. On the afternoon of our last day aboard the ship, we were on deck visiting with other passengers when the announcement circulated that we had passed the border between Brazil and Uruguay. We quickly made our way to the side of the ship straining our eyes for a glimpse of land. A man loaned us his binoculars through which we observed the distant shoreline. A number of hours passed and darkness came. The ship entered the Rio de la Plata, and soon we could see a shimmering sea of lights shining across the water. Our ship became stuck in the shallow waters of the port. For four hours, small boats struggled to free us from the mud. I believe that the Lord allowed this delay to occur so that my dad would have the opportunity to gather my mother and me at the rail of the ship and talk with us about the thousands of souls waiting on the distant shore to hear the gospel. He reassured us that the Lord would be our Light, and that He had called us to be His light to those people whom He loves as much as He loves you and me.

Finally, just before midnight our ship was secured at the dock. My mother, my daddy, and I disembarked together from the comfort zone of that American ship into a life of total dependence upon the all-sufficient grace of Jesus. What kind of grace? The grace which enables one to learn a new language and culture, to share with unbelievers their need of salvation, and to weather the storms that Satan inevitably sends.

Jesus truly became my Light. Until that moment Jesus had been my salvation for three years, since the age of nine. But I had not truly recognized Him as my Light, the One Who could guide me through each day regardless of the circumstances. Mother and Daddy had been my light. This would not be possible in the world I had entered. I would have to learn to look to Jesus as my Light. He was willing and waiting. I found Him to be more than sufficient.

How sufficient was His grace? It was so sufficient that the love and burden He placed in my heart for the people of Uruguay burn as deeply in my heart today as they did in those formative years.

His grace was so sufficient that all the forces of hell that Satan has marshaled over almost four decades to destroy the work of BMAA missions in Uruguay have utterly failed. How faithful He has been!

His grace was so sufficient that many who have come to know Jesus through the ministry of missions in Uruguay now live eternally in heaven. What a God of victory we serve!

We must grow in His grace to the point that our course is charted by His will, our actions are energized by the fruits of the Spirit, and our view of the world is actually His own operating within us. Only then will we be qualified to serve as vessels from which His love will be poured into the lives of lost people around the world. He is waiting to mold each of us into the servant He would have us to be. Are we ready to join in the prayer of Isaiah 64:8, *"But now, O LORD, thou art our father; we are the clay, and thou our potter; and we all are the work of thy hand"?* Are we willing for Him to fashion us into His vessels? Will we answer yes?

God's people must heed His voice lest we stand guilty before Him of the blood of millions who vacillate without hope in confusion and spiritual despair. Brother and Mrs. Wayne Ely, missionaries to Honduras, encounter such need in every corner of the field to which they have been called. They are touched daily by the plight of people such as one particular lady whose testimony they share.

Jesús, a single mother of five from La Entrada, Copan, admonishes all who hear her testimony to look to Christ. She expresses her deep gratitude that Christ came to her when she needed Him in the most difficult moments of her life. This time was when her heart was most open to the gospel.

Jesús had reached a point of hopelessness; she felt her life had no meaning. She became disinterested in her children and certainly cared nothing for their father. She felt she could not survive under the burden of providing and caring for five children alone. Her depression became so severe that she would collapse into tears in the presence of her children.

Just when Jesús felt she had reached the end of her strength, she heard the gospel. Hearing the message of salvation she responded as a starving soul which hungers and thirsts for hope. She describes the change that Christ brought in her life as beautiful and extraordinary. Her testimony has resulted in the salvation of four of her children. She credits God's infinite love for the happiness and peace that now reign in her home. After following the Lord in baptism, she has grown in her knowledge of the Word and in her faith.

She testifies that her life since her salvation has not been without difficulty and pain. Within the last year she has lost her beloved mother. She has depended upon the all-sufficient comfort of her Lord to fill this vacuum in her heart. She faces each day in the forgiveness, love, and hope of her heavenly Father.

Missionaries John David and Kim Smith serve along with Chris Shaw in the Cape Verde Islands. They encounter many people whose spiritual condition vividly illustrates the concept that must motivate all of us daily. Lost people must hear the truth before they can believe. Irondina is a young convert in their ministry who spent her youth fervently trusting in her good works to enable her to earn eternal life. Upon hearing the scriptures which so clearly describe God's grace as the only source of salvation, she was convicted by the Holy Spirit to receive Christ. Her ignorance was replaced by a hunger and thirst for the Word of God which cannot be quenched. The power of His truth is released by fervent prayer!

Reflect, Discuss & Apply

1. What steps can you take to increase your awareness of how many people in your community, state, nation, and on foreign fields have still not heard the gospel?

   _____

   _____

   _____

2. How can you discover the Lord's will for your personal place of service in His great plan for the work of missions?

3. What can you do each day to surrender to His calling upon your life for the work of missions?

4. How can you increase your burden for lost souls individually, whether you are personally acquainted with them or not, without regard to race, creed, or status in life?

5. How can you participate in training children to understand the importance of missions work?

6. What can you do to encourage and support servants of the Lord who have been called directly to be missionaries on the local, state, national, and international fields of service?

8

BY OUR OBEDIENCE

One day we shall stand in the presence of almighty God to give account of our obedience to His Word. In that moment our selfish personal goals will melt away before the awesome reality that only what we allowed Christ to accomplish in our lives is eternal. We will see so clearly that the soul's eternal condition is infinitely more important than the condition or appearance of our earthly bodies.

We must believe in the power of God to change lives. Satan attempts to break our resolve with the deception that missions makes no real difference and isn't worth the time, money, or effort required. He particularly wants us to believe that it is useless to devote a lifetime career to missions work. Americans are particularly susceptible to this deceit because of our tendency to believe that because there are so many churches in our nation all have heard the gospel.

Sadly, many believers never take the time to challenge Satan's lie. We are able to discover firsthand how God has changed lives when communities hear the gospel. Testimonies from abroad move us to support missionaries in distant places and to renew our commitment to those hopeless lost souls around us.

Our mission would be far less challenging if obedience to the Lord's command could be as simple as aligning our will with the Lord's and moving ahead. But when we make our decision to obey, we are marching into battle. Satan is determined to wage war against the mission to win souls. At every turn he is there to oppose the salvation of a soul. He is the greatest enemy to the mission we must fulfill. For this reason, the Lord gave us the assurance that *"Ye are of God, little children, and have overcome them* [all evil spirits]*: because greater is he that is in you, than he that is in the world"* (1 John 4:4).

The apostle Paul was intensely and personally familiar with the warfare of being a missionary for the Lord. He admonished the Ephesians to *"put on the whole armour of God, that ye may be able to stand against the wiles of the devil"* (Ephesians 6:11). He listed in Ephesians 6:14-17 the components of this armor as critical elements in our warfare. Our armor includes truth, righteousness, the gospel, faith, salvation, and the sword of the Spirit (the Word).

Unfortunately we harbor the hope that if we persist in our labor, then Satan will give up attacking us; or that a victory over his attack in one instance will prevent him from assaulting us again. When he continues to batter us, we become discouraged. The Bible provides us with many accounts of people dedicated to God's calling who battled Satan to the very end of their lives. God's plan requires that we put on the whole armor of God and go forth in the battle for souls in His strength. He overcomes Satan's vicious attacks in ways that we find miraculous and supernatural. In so doing, He strengthens our faith. Remember that the victories the Lord gives are not confined to our finite understanding. While we desire victories immediately, the Lord may patiently work with people or situations for years to bring about His will. It is critical that we remind ourselves constantly that our responsibility is obedience. The architect of victory is the Lord! For Paul this truth was enough. Though he found himself in bonds, his desire was not diminished as he begged the Ephesians to pray *"that utterance may be given unto me, that I may open my mouth boldly, to make known the mystery of the gospel"* (6:19).

Satan seeks to hinder missions by distracting believers from God's plan of spreading the gospel. Unless we are committed to our part in the whole plan, we are not fully obedient. Jesus spoke of witnesses in Jerusalem, Judea, Samaria, and unto the uttermost part of the earth. He was describing individual and corporate responsibility for witnessing where one lives and carrying the gospel to the entire world. We tend not to see ourselves as a vital part of each of these fields. Many temptations blind us in one or more of these areas. We may diligently witness to lost people around us, but feel no duty to support missionary efforts in distant fields with our prayers and giving. On the other hand, we may contribute to missions endeavors on one or more levels, while passing lost people every day without mentioning the name of Jesus to them.

We may also be tempted to excuse ourselves from personal involvement by assuring ourselves that our church is contributing to missions on various levels. The church was given the Great Commission by Jesus, *"Go ye therefore, and teach all nations, baptizing them in the name of the Father, and of the Son, and of the Holy Ghost: teaching them to observe all things whatsoever I have commanded you"* (Matthew 28:19-20). But we are the components of our church. You and I have personally received the command of missions. We are personally responsible for implementing His divine plan to share the gospel with souls across the world. That is both a privilege and a sobering challenge!

Obedience to the Lord's will often calls for a total change in the direction of individual lives. There are countless examples of this truth in the pages of scripture. Consider Noah, Moses and Aaron, David, the Twelve whom Jesus chose, the apostle Paul, and all those who have followed in their footsteps throughout the centuries. Turning from lives of sin to salvation, they were instantly called to fully surrender to the Lord's mission. We share the same call even though we often languish in halfhearted commitment. Many men and women have lived in times when mediocre commitment was not an option. Their situations and their faith sharpened their focus and sealed their commitment. Others have grown to adulthood in a society relatively free of Christian persecution and have been called to missionary service in completely unexpected circumstances. Our task is to be so attuned to the daily guidance of the Holy Spirit that we will not miss His call, even if it comes in the most ordinary moment and in the most familiar surroundings. My father's testimony of his call from the Lord to be a missionary illustrates this important fact.

Daddy was born and raised on a farm in the small rural community of Grice, located in northeast Texas. His family was active in the Antioch Baptist Church during the years of the Depression, when church services were held monthly. Revival times in the summer were the highlight of the spiritual life of the people, because this was a time set aside to focus upon spiritual matters, and typically many were saved on these occasions.

These Christian people lived their daily lives trusting the Lord for sustenance and instilling faith in their children. They fulfilled the command of missions among their children and their neighbors. Visits from missionaries on distant fields were almost unknown.

When my father joined the Navy to serve in World War II, he experienced his first view of other parts of his country and the world. At this time he was still unsaved. He wrestled with his own spiritual condition until after the war when at the age of twenty-one, in 1947, he gave his heart to the Lord in a Sunday morning worship service in Dallas.

Daddy became active in his home church in his beloved northeast Texas community and began to make his living in various jobs. He married my mother, Allyne Morris, shortly after he took office as the clerk of Upshur County.

Soon Daddy began to feel the call of the Lord to the ministry. He had many ambitions and plans, all of which were incompatible with being a preacher. He discovered that the Lord can change circumstances at staggering speed. When the Korean Conflict began to escalate, he was called back into the Navy. While serving on a ship in the waters off the shore of Korea, he surrendered to the Lord's call to the ministry. In a matter of days he found himself disembarking from the ship in Japan. The Lord showed him a grassy knoll located a few yards away from the center of activity, and in the short free moment that he had he climbed over the knoll, fell to his knees, and prayed that the Lord would allow him to return home safely to follow His calling. As he returned to his quarters, orders were being given over the public address system. He listened in amazement as his name was read from a list of those designated to be immediately transferred stateside by plane to be discharged from the Navy.

During ten years of pastorate at two churches, from 1954-1964, my father's ministry was blessed. He began to read accounts of missions work in state and national publications such as the *Gleaner*. He began to lead his church to pray for missionaries, to contribute to missions, to send messengers to state and national associational meetings, to participate in the organization of local missions churches, and to invite missionaries to his church to speak. He was truly interested in all the fields and especially enjoyed being personally involved in local missions endeavors. He was a bivocational pastor, teaching sixth grade and serving as principal in an elementary school. He had begun to feel the Lord leading him to serve as a missionary, but he had no idea where he should begin. One afternoon he was preparing a social studies lesson for his sixth-grade class. He opened the textbook to a chapter on South America. There before him was a picture of a Uruguayan pasture with a gaucho tending his flock of sheep. Below the picture was a brief column of basic information on this tiny, obscure country. The still small voice of the Holy Spirit was firm and sure. The Lord had chosen for Daddy to carry the gospel to the people of Uruguay. In spite of many questions there was no denial and no turning back. The Lord confirmed His call in innumerable and unmistakable ways.

How does one make the physical and cultural transition from rural East Texas to Uruguay to carry the gospel? How do you get from wherever you are today to the center of His will for your life as His missionary? That is entirely impossible for us, but entirely possible for the Lord. We make that journey by following each step in the footprint of Christ as He walks ahead of us preparing the way. This is our journey. The road traverses valleys and climbs mountains physically and spiritually. It holds dangers, challenges, and infinite blessings. Our decision of whether or not to say yes to the Lord will impact the lives of countless other people. My father chose to say yes. As a result many Uruguayan souls are now in heaven with him and, best of all, with the Lord. Because he chose to say yes, my life as his daughter was forever impacted spiritually. His decision provided me with a priceless opportunity to watch the Lord work as only He can.

Only in eternity will we know how many lives are impacted by our decision to answer the Lord's call upon our lives. In addition to my life, my dad's decision to obey the call of the Lord impacted the lives of people whom he did not meet during his tenure as a missionary, but whom the Lord was preparing for the gospel and for service. The Lord's directing of events in the lives of people and the timing of those events are never a mistake. Consider the testimony of a faithful family whom the Lord has used as national missionaries for more than three decades.

On July 11, 1963, a baby was born to Ruben and Hortensia Reyes of Montevideo, Uruguay. It was deep winter in this very southern corner of South America. Ruben, age thirty-nine, and Hortensia, age thirty-eight, had waited eighteen years for the birth of this son, who would be their only child.

The baby's name was still in doubt following his birth. Though not yet born-again Christians, Hortensia was an avid student of the Bible, and she was partial to the book of Ezekiel. She expressed her desire to name the boy Ezekiel, but was persuaded by friends that the name would appear too Jewish so she agreed to Daniel.

The family's delight over the birth of the long-awaited Daniel would soon be interrupted by what appeared at the time to be a devastating event. Ruben was involved in a very serious car accident. News of his death was carried on radio in Montevideo. Actually clinging to life, he was transferred to a hospital with more sophisticated surgical facilities where he underwent a lengthy and difficult operation. His family was given virtually no hope for his recovery, but the Lord had other plans. After three days of unconsciousness, he awoke asking for a Bible.

Though Ruben's physical recovery was lengthy, the resulting spiritual journey proved to be pivotal. For seven years the family settled into their routine daily life, but Ruben's heart had been irreversibly opened to the Word. In early 1970, just three months after missionary James Poole had returned to the United States from the field in Uruguay, a national pastor chose to witness to Ruben in the workplace they shared.

Soon the Reyes family began attending the Good Shepherd Missionary Baptist Church. They received

Christ as Savior and were baptized. Ruben immediately dedicated himself so fully to the church that he was soon ordained as a deacon. He served two years, during which time he surrendered to the ministry. He was ordained a pastor in 1972. Beginning in 1973 he served the First Missionary Baptist Church of Estacion Atlantida as pastor for twenty years. He also directed the BMAA mission work in Uruguay.

In 1974, Ruben enjoyed the special blessing of baptizing ten-year-old Daniel. Daniel became his father's constant companion and right arm in the mission work while continuing to pursue a very rigorous academic track in school. During a visit by former missionary James Poole in 1980, seventeen-year-old Daniel felt particularly impressed that his future lay in the missionary ministry of the Uruguayan churches.

In 1981, Daniel was scheduled to take the entrance exams to the College of Law of the University of the Oriental Republic of Uruguay. Daniel had never wavered from his belief that this was the Lord's will for his life, that his education would become an invaluable tool in his ministry. No one who knew Daniel's academic ability and record had any doubt that he would pass the entrance exams without difficulty. When sufficient time had passed for the results of the exams to be posted in the office, Daniel decided to go and find his name on the list of those who had passed. Unbelievably it wasn't there.

For days he languished in disoriented shock not knowing which direction to turn. One afternoon while taking a long walk to try and sort out his dilemma, Daniel passed by a school of linguistics where several languages are taught. He thought that it would be wise to spend the year studying French and Italian, which would be very useful in future legal studies. At least he would not waste the year of waiting to take the entrance exams again.

As a result of enrolling in classes to study Italian Daniel became acquainted with a number of people in the Italian community and found work with his newly-acquired language. He also met Maria Cecilia Tornaria, the young lady the Lord had chosen for his wife.

There are no *what ifs* in the Lord's kingdom. If Daniel had passed his first entrance exams, he might never have enrolled in the language school or learned Italian. He then would never have become acquainted with friends in the Italian community, and thus might have missed one of God's greatest blessings in his life, his faithful wife Cecilia. Even more importantly, Cecilia might never have heard the gospel. We truly serve an awesome God.

Meanwhile Daniel had passed the entrance exams on his second attempt. He and Cecilia began attending the university together, and she was saved and baptized in 1985. Daniel publicly surrendered to the ministry and was ordained on January 19, 1986, to become assistant pastor to his father. In August, 1987, he accepted the pastorate of the Good Shepherd Church following a four-month trip to the United States where he visited churches and worked at the Center of Life in Houston, Texas.

Upon returning to Uruguay Daniel resumed his studies and graduated from Law School in 1988. Daniel and Cecilia were marred on June 6, 1989, and she subsequently graduated with her law degree. Since this time, they have faithfully served as national missionaries of the BMAA, and have watched in amazement as the Lord has used their legal profession to facilitate the work of the ministry in Uruguay. Their daughter, Maria Victoria, is very active in the ministry and is a special blessing to her elderly grandparents Ruben and Hortensia. In their seventies, they are retired BMAA national missionaries, but are still very faithful in the church they have served for so long.

Daniel reflects upon his journey with the Lord with these words, "It seems just yesterday that the Lord saved our souls. We continue the journey serving in the vineyard, and may the children of today, as we did, become the servants of tomorrow."

Will you say yes to the Lord's call upon your life? You, your family, and those to whom you minister the gospel will be eternally touched by the Lord's power as a result.

Reflect, Discuss & Apply

1. Read Proverbs 11:30. List the names of lost persons with whom you have spoken about salvation within the last month, year, or a period of time of your choosing.
2. What can you do to walk in the wisdom described by this verse?
3. Read the book of Jonah. What are the consequences of disobeying the will of God? How can you obey God's voice and do your part to spread the gospel?
4. Acknowledge that God does not honor half-hearted obedience to His will. What should be your life priorities according to Matthew 6:19-21?
5. Describe Jesus' example of obedience as recorded in Matthew 26:39.
6. List priorities in your life that the Holy Spirit is convicting you to reorder. What activities or habits are hindering your complete obedience to the Lord's will for you as His servant? Pray for the Lord's help to claim Philippians 4:13 as you allow Him to mold you as His vessel.
7. What can you do to improve the future effectiveness of your church's missions ministry by obedience to the Lord's command found in Mark 16:15?

9

BY OUR PRAYER

A missionary's most critical need is a faithful prayer partner. We must not neglect this need as we seek to fulfill our commission. Before we can carry out any aspect of the Great Commission, we must saturate the endeavor with unrelenting prayer. Time spent in the presence of the Lord accompanied by the Holy Spirit is the source of our strength, courage, and ability. Lacking prayer we are unequipped, unempowered, and unprepared. While exhorting the Ephesians to put on the armor of God, the apostle Paul emphasized that they should go forward into the harvest of souls *"praying always with all prayer and supplication in the Spirit"* (Ephesians 6:18). He instructed the Romans to be servants that are *"rejoicing in hope; patient in tribulation; continuing instant in prayer"* (Romans 12:12).

The Lord often uses great trials to equip His chosen servants. The Lord can use the very circumstances we find so difficult to effectively carry His Word further into our journey.

Myint Aung was born into a large family of Christians who practiced their faith in name only. In 1958, when he was in second grade, his family migrated to Burma, now Myanmar. Time passed, and Myint was chosen to study in the capital city of Rangoon. At age thirteen he entered a school run by Buddhist missionaries. These missionaries promised the parents of their prospective students that they would receive an excellent education, preparing them well for life.

In what turned out to be a monastery, the monks educated the children in Buddhist thought and ideology. They were sent to day schools for secular education. Throughout his youth, Myint lived in the monastery and was schooled in Buddhism. He graduated with a degree in geology from Rangoon University. By this time the truths he had heard in Christian Sunday School as a child had been erased by his intense training as a Buddhist. His whole life had been conformed to Buddhism. This sad condition was about to be radically changed by the power of God.

In 1973, a group of young believers arrived on the university campus to witness. In student fellowship meetings they shared powerful testimonies about Jesus. Myint had been warned never to associate with Christians or listen to their teachings. Myint knew that the destiny of the road his life was taking would lead him to be a Buddhist priest. He knew that he had reached a crossroads in which he must make the most critical decision of his life. Myint praises God that he chose Christianity, leaving behind the indoctrination he had embraced even though at that moment he did not yet have a full understanding of personal salvation.

During the years of Myint's education, his family lived seven hundred miles to the north of Rangoon. Communication and transportation were extremely poor — so difficult that he had not received news of the deaths of both his parents. Upon hearing this news and having left the monastery, Myint knew that he would face a struggle just to survive financially.

A soldier's family took Myint into their home until he could make other living arrangements. He found work in a hotel, but was forced to spend so many hours earning so little pay that his education virtually stopped. In 1976, the Lord sent a Christian girl named Mal Sawmi into Myint's life. She devoted herself to helping Myint finish his education.

More importantly Mal prayed that Myint would truly be converted. Her prayer was gloriously answered on July 5, 1978, when the witness of many friends, pastors, and evangelists resulted in Myint giving his heart to Christ. He was immediately burdened to share his faith with others like himself who had been exposed to mediocre Christian teaching in their childhood, but who had never really been taught concepts such as *being born again* or *conversion*.

The Lord has brought Myint and Mal through many experiences, including study at the BMAA Seminary, in their preparation to serve as missionaries in their country of Myanmar. Our commitment to prayer for the cause of missions should never waver. We do not know where the Lord is raising up His next generation of servants. They need our diligent prayer.

Diligent prayer is often required to penetrate hearts and extract people from the false teachings of ingrained religions. Yet another testimony of the power of prayer in such cases is that of John Adam. He is the oldest son of Adam and Marianna Kuntonkori, devout Muslims from Sokodie in northern Togo, Africa. John's paternal grandparents had settled in Ghana, in a village called Ayaasu, around the turn of the century. The couple raised their children making a living as farm laborers. In the 1950s, the daughter of devout Muslim neighbors, a girl named Marianna, was given in marriage to their son Adam, as is customary in Muslim homes.

There was never any question in the Kuntonkori home that John would follow all the traditions of his family's religion. After all, he was the first-born son, and was considered next of kin to his father. He did not even attend school since this would mean exposure to other religions.

John was raised in all the traditions of Muhammad and learned to perform all the required Muslim rituals.

He became a *Koratu*, or teacher of children. He married and moved to Offinso where he became a night keeper at the cocoa storage shed. He practiced his rituals faithfully, sacrificing small gods for his sins, and praying five times for forgiveness as he confessed them.

Hard times befell the cocoa shed where John was employed, and he prayed earnestly to Allah that he would not lose his job. His prayer was not answered. In disillusionment and desperation, he informed his father, Adam, that he was leaving his Muslim religion because it was empty and not good for his three children. This decision resulted in John's loss of his wife, who was taken from him by forced divorce.

With the severance pay he received from his job, John built a house. A wealthy cocoa farmer assisted John and invited him to his church to find God. When John's family heard the news that he had attended a church of another faith, they cursed him and began to make his life even more difficult. He continued to attend the church for ten years, never experiencing a real change. He found that simply fulfilling another set of religious rituals did not yield the peace he sought.

On January 10, 1997, a tenant in John's house overheard a bitter quarrel between John and his wife, with whom he had been restored. He invited John to accompany him to an open-air evangelistic service, if for no other reason than to calm his anger. John testifies that, "Jesus was there waiting for me." Following a film on the Rapture, a message was preached. Before the invitation was given John hurried to the altar, fell to his knees, and cried out for salvation. He was gloriously saved.

For eleven months, he was able to demonstrate his new faith before his elderly father, who was dying. The old man could not escape the evident change in John and advised all his children to come to John to seek the truth he had found. He told John to hold fast to the

Jesus he had received in his heart. As he lay dying, he asked John to pray for him. John's salvation was the direct result of God's everlasting faithfulness.

Many missionaries confront people who are committed to certain religious traditions out of the stark reality of financial need and other difficult challenges. Such was the case in a testimony shared from Costa Rica by veteran missionaries Duane and Francis Heflin. In the town of San Lorenzo they became acquainted with a young widow who had no means to support her four children. The only solution she could find was to enroll her two older daughters in a charitable religious school. In this setting they were provided shelter in dormitories and meals. Along with receiving their physical needs, they were schooled in all the prerequisite training to take lifelong positions of service in that religion.

While the girls were living at the school their mother was invited to the Baptist church where she soon accepted Christ as Savior. On holiday from school, the girls arrived home to find their mother changed. They thoroughly enjoyed attending Vacation Bible School and Sunday School. During their time at home each of the sisters trusted Christ for salvation, but they soon had to return to school. Though required by their circumstances to remain in the school for a period of time, they never wavered from their newfound faith and began to grow in the Lord. As teenagers, they were able to leave the school and return home, where they served the Lord faithfully in their church in San Lorenzo. They enrolled in Bible institute to prepare to be better servants of the Lord. Their testimony amplifies our understanding of the beloved verse, *"And ye shall know the truth, and the truth shall make you free"* (John 8:32). Jesus can release us from whatever physical, emotional, or spiritual stronghold exists in our life. How we need to convey that message across the world!

Reflect, Discuss & Apply

1. Begin a prayer journal and record your prayers for lost souls, for your own witness, and for missionaries witnessing to souls you cannot reach.
2. Read Ephesians 6:18-19. Paul earnestly pleaded with the Ephesians to pray for him that he would have boldness to preach the gospel. He also admonished them to pray for all their brothers and sisters in Christ, fellow missionaries of the gospel. In your prayer journal list the people you will commit to pray for daily.
3. Consider the admonitions given in 1 Thessalonians 5:17 and Hebrews 13:18. How can you cultivate such a continuous attitude of prayer?

   _____

   _____

4. Read James 5:16-17 which assures us of the effectiveness of prayer. What can you do to claim this promise and follow this example?

   _____

   _____

   _____

5. Use the prayer calendars that appear in the *Gleaner** and the prayer calendar booklets that are distributed in preparation for World Missions Sunday to design a personal daily prayer plan.
6. Resolve to spend time in prayer daily on behalf of these people, their needs, and what the Lord would have you do to help them.

*The *Gleaner* is the bimonthly missions magazine published by the Baptist Missionary Association of America missions agency. To subscribe call 501-455-4977.

10

BY OUR PERSEVERANCE

Many missionaries face the curse of alcoholism in the lives of the people they serve. Men, particularly, pass their misery on to innocent families in an unending cycle of suffering. People offer poverty, peer pressure, and many other excuses to explain their fall to Satan's devices which paralyzes sound judgment and brings tragic consequences.

Ricardo, a young Mexican father, is a portrait of effective missions, when persistence and prayer work hand in hand with the movement of the Holy Spirit. Ricardo fell into a lifestyle which revolved around daily drinking with friends and the neglect of his family. His life spiraled downward into an abyss from which he would never recover. He lost control of himself and his family relationship. No doubt he would have eventually lost his health and his life. His wife, Yolanda, responded to her circumstances by becoming a mean-spirited and bitter individual. Her plight affected her ability to create a loving home or to be the caring and committed school teacher she needed to be.

Through the witness of a Christian colleague and the faithful prayers of a missions-minded church, Yolanda read of God's love and salvation, attended a Bible study, and came to know Christ as her personal Savior. Her life changed immediately. She began to pray fervently for Ricardo. She could easily have given up as matters only grew worse. But one day through her prayer and the witness of missionary John Ladd and counselor Carlos Cano, Ricardo heard about Christ and accepted Him as Savior. His life since that time is a testament to 2 Corinthians 5:17, *"Therefore if any man be in Christ, he is a new creature: old things are passed away; behold, all things are become new."*

Ricardo was led by the Holy Spirit to stop selling alcoholic beverages and to use the money from the sale of his existing stock of beer to have the road of the church improved. He has served in subsequent years in many capacities in his church, and is the leader of a mountain mission to the Huastecan people. Best of all, he is a living witness to the power of Jesus Christ to transform lives. His story inspires us to go and tell, no matter how unlikely the outcome may seem.

Our source of strength to persevere is always the Lord. He provides us with wisdom and encourages us through others' testimonies of victory over adversity. Their personal testimonies show how we can trust God in our own difficult circumstances. Scripture gives us numerous accounts of people who persevered in their calling in the face of great adversity. Two beloved examples are Daniel and Esther. Daniel was called to show his unwavering faith as a prayer warrior. Esther was called to save her people by facing a king. Many believers throughout the ages have risen to persevere in adversity by faith.

Brother Travis McPeek, who has now gone to be with the Lord, shared such a testimony that has strengthened the faith of my church. From the history of the Enon Church, he related the story of a night in 1934 when word spread throughout our rural community that the church building was burning. As the heartbroken members gathered to watch in helpless horror, their beloved building with its imposing steeple, the centerpiece of the community, burned to the ground. Penniless in this time of a depressed economy, the prospects for finding resources to rebuild were very bleak. But these men and women were very intimately familiar with Psalm 121, particularly verses one and two, in which the Psalmist exclaimed with deep conviction, *"I will lift up mine eyes unto the hills, from whence cometh my help. My help cometh from the LORD, which made heaven and earth."* There in the cold by the light of the burning embers, as Brother Travis recalled, the families of Enon church joined arms beside the smoldering ruins and prayed, vowing to rebuild their church building by the strength and provision of the Lord. The Lord blessed their efforts, and the building they built is still being used today, having been donated in the spirit of missions to another congregation when the current Enon church building was built.

The apostle Paul often admonished believers to stand fast, to persevere, and to follow his example to *"press toward the mark for the prize of the high calling of God in Christ Jesus"* (Philippians 3:14). We are the beneficiaries of the fact that Paul did exactly what He said. He was, after all, a missionary to the Gentiles. His faithfulness and that of many others brought us the gospel. Others across the world who hunger and thirst for the gospel await our faithfulness and perseverance.

Missionaries persevere because of their love for their Savior, His church and its commission, lost souls, and their calling. I have never heard a missionary proclaim that the work is easy. I have also never heard a missionary offer to exchange the work of God for any other career.

Believers discover great joy in finding God's perfect will and persevering in His calling. Christ's call always involves being a missionary to someone and sharing the good news of salvation with the lost.

Our perseverance doesn't depend on numbers of converts or building impressive facilities. It is a lifestyle, to be lived by the guidance of the Holy Spirit in our hearts. The greatest victories in life often occur after lengthy periods of struggle and prayer. We must show the world

By Our Perseverance

that nothing can deter us from the path of faithfulness. A world of lost, eternity-bound souls awaits our witness. God will prevail. Will we persevere?

Perhaps the most experienced witnesses in this matter of perseverance are those who have ministered in countries formerly behind the Iron Curtain. Brother and Mrs. Jeff Franks, Brother and Mrs. Heith Youngblood, Miss Laura Marsh, and many national missionaries face the challenges of witnessing to people who have lived in the realities of a repressive regime. Brother Fiodor Baraniuk has shared many of these living stories of victory.

Victor Kopitin was born in the town of Voronezh, Russia. He grew up believing that he would find his life's destiny in the world of sports. One nagging, persistent question prevented his heart from being totally fulfilled and happy. He desperately needed to know the meaning of life. Having reached manhood, he dutifully entered military service only to find no answers to his search for truth. He felt a great desire to act upon the struggle he was experiencing. He sought happiness in all the usual life events, his marriage at age twenty-two and the birth of his daughter. These blessings did not quench the spiritual thirst of his soul.

Sadly, Victor turned to the counterfeit glory of crime. He was imprisoned for four years, during which he read a great deal of literature in his search for truth. Upon his release from prison his family accepted him with grace, and he and his wife soon had a son. He would search the night skies with his eyes pondering the emptiness of his soul, but he could not see "...the star of Bethlehem." Soon he fell back into crime and was sentenced to six more years of confinement.

Victor tried to pray to God for help, but he had no idea of the love of Jesus. He received a New Testament from a Christian group and, while reading it, felt convicted that its story was what he needed. Then the book was lost, and Victor became very sick for several months. He prayed very hard that he could find another New Testament. His relatives were able to bring him one on a visit. Upon receiving it, Victor prayed the sinner's prayer, repenting in tears of his sins and receiving Jesus into his heart.

Victor was a new creation in Christ with new attitudes, speech, and actions. For the following six years, he witnessed for Christ in prison. He won at least a dozen inmates to Christ.

Victor's marriage had ended in divorce, but through much prayer, Victor's wife recognized the change in his life and agreed to remarry. Soon after the ceremony was conducted in the prison, Victor's wife was saved. A third child was born to their union.

Following Victor's release from prison, he began a ministry of evangelism in area prisons surrounding his home town. He is now a missionary and directs a prison ministry outreach from his church in Voronezh. He reaches out to prisoners with the eternal hope of a forgiving Savior who has the power to change defeat and despair into hope and victory.

Suppose for a moment that those who delivered the New Testaments to the prisons had given up, deciding that the personal risk was too great, that the prospect of converting criminals was too bleak. Thank God for those who persevere in His name no matter the cost.

Often those who must endure ridicule and rejection as they follow Christ need encouragement. Maria faced the imminent death of her beloved husband, Peter, with great fear and sorrow. She turned to her friends for comfort, but, like many who have no eternal hope, they were uncomfortable with her plight and avoided her.

A believer named Valya heard of Peter's terminal condition and came to witness to him about Jesus. Peter's heart was open, and he asked Valya to return regularly to read to him from the Bible.

As Peter's physical strength ebbed, he faced the most important decision of his life. One evening as Valya shared the scriptures, Peter summoned his last bit of physical energy, rose from his bed, and knelt with Valya. He confessed his sins to Jesus and accepted Him as his personal Savior. He died with the peace of Jesus in his heart and on his face.

Maria took great comfort in this experience. However, at Peter's death she had to make some difficult decisions. In the culture of that country a reception is held at the time of burial called a *pominski*. It is considered rude not to offer alcoholic beverages to the guests. She was torn between her respect for her husband's views against drinking and the traditions of her people. In her husband's memory she decided that she should be loyal to God, so she made preparations for a meal of the best food possible, but no alcohol.

The guests arrived for the reception and enjoyed the delicious food for an hour. As is the custom, they began to flick their glasses indicating that they were ready for the vodka. When told that there would be none, they began to shame and berate Maria.

Maria began to attend believers' meetings in her town of Nikolaevka where she was saved and baptized. She could not leave her apartment, however, without her neighbors jeering and calling her a *traitor*. One told her how much she hated her, to which Maria responded in love.

According to tradition a *pominski* is held once again on the first anniversary of the death of a loved one. As the time approached for Peter's second *pominski*, Maria invited all her friends and neighbors. At her request, her pastor shared the gospel and how it had changed Peter's eternal destiny. When he had finished, the people began to quietly leave. No one knew if they did this from embarrassment or because there was no alcohol to drink.

In the succeeding days, Maria found out that one man who had been present had spent all night contemplating the sermon while another expressed interest in attending a gospel meeting. In addition, the verbal abuse and criticism of Maria abruptly ended. Soon Maria's church held a holiday celebration to which they invited the public for a musical concert and scripture recitations by children. More than one hundred and fifty of the community attended. What an impact Maria's series of courageous decisions had on spreading the gospel in Nikolaevka. Are we equally bold in using every opportunity to spread the gospel?

Reflect, Discuss & Apply

1. Perseverance is one of the most difficult challenges to witnesses and missionaries. Read Romans 8:26-27, and 31. What do these verses promise which will enable believers to stand in the face of testing?

2. List some ways we can encourage missionaries.

3. Ask your study group to compile a list of people they have been praying to see saved. Commit to help each other persevere in prayer.
4. How can you support and resolve to participate in the cause of worldwide missions?

11

BY OUR GIVING

God uses many tools to meet lost people at their point of need. He sends people into the harvest. He sends the message out by radio, television, computer technology, literature, and other means.

Satan seeks to deceive us into believing that our missions support is ineffective and irrelevant. He has made every effort to sabotage the use of modern technology to spread the gospel. He has attempted to convince us that the printing, distribution, and recycling of literature is useless. From Ghana, West Africa, come testimonies that resoundingly disprove his deceit. The name of the village of *Domeabra* means, "If you love me, you will come." That name alone should convince us of the urgency of missions. The Bible Baptist Church in this village consists of typically gentle, loving African people who love the Lord and desire to see their countrymen saved. One Sunday morning service illustrates what a gravely important place gospel literature fills in missions, especially when most people do not own Bibles. Nine people accepted Christ through the study of a Sunday School lesson on John 3:16. The lesson opened the hearts of people who have been exposed throughout life to the culture of witch doctors and idol worship. God's Word was then proclaimed by missionary John Lindsey, and lives were changed. We must send the gospel into the world through every means the Lord provides.

Believers in Christ know that the Lord owns *"the cattle upon a thousand hills"* (Psalm 50:10). He owns everything because He created everything. Unfortunately we sometimes try to apply the principle of self-sufficiency and independence to spiritual matters. While hard work and earning one's living are scriptural principles, the fruit of our labor is not due to our own strength. Whatever we possess truly belongs to God which He has provided through his mercy and generosity. We have the opportunity to honor Him with our giving and service.

Giving is an important act of worship, an expression of gratitude and praise. God created our act of giving as another tool by which we could participate in spreading the gospel. It is awesome to consider that God can take our meager gifts and send the gospel to souls across the world. God can multiply a young lad's loaves and fishes or a widow's mite. He can place coins in the mouths of fish. He can replenish oil and flour. He can use our offerings to carry out His work in the lives of people we will never meet until eternity. The material possessions of this world cannot bring us the eternal joy that comes from helping to finance the spread of the gospel.

Satan seeks to ensnare us and hinder our giving by appealing to a false sense of financial responsibility. He tempts us to judge how God's money is spent and to entangle ourselves with endless questions about whether money is being spent on fruitful missions efforts. Few of us will ever enjoy the opportunity to visit every mission field we have the privilege of supporting financially. Such an opportunity would humble us by the vast need for the gospel, inspire us by the dedication of the missionary workers, and shame us for our lack of sacrifice. As God honors those who manage His affairs with loving care and concern, He expects us to honor those whom He has called with our trust. He is the judge of both their service and our giving. What a privilege God has given us to participate in spreading the gospel through our giving.

Satan also seeks to control our use of the Lord's gift of time. He deludes us into believing that our time is ours to use as we please. We plan our days as if we were the architects of time. God asks that we acknowledge Him as the Creator of time, that we recognize His purpose for each day of our lives, and that we use our time according to His will. When time no longer exists (Revelation 10:6) and our time for service is gone forever, will we be judged as good stewards of the time He has given us?

God has also blessed us with gifts and talents that He can use to make us effective witnesses. We must realize that these belong to the Lord. Without Him we are nothing. Whatever abilities He has enabled us to develop are meant for service. In our society we hear much about fulfillment in life. The Christian finds fulfillment in service. God wants to cultivate within you and me a servant's heart. Only then will we willingly and cheerfully surrender our resources to His will. First, we must place ourselves on the altar. He awaits our decision.

Eternity rewards such a decision with transformed lives. For the Buddy Johnson family, this decision became a daily journey as they served in the region of Huejutla, Mexico. Their ministry to the Olivares family conveys the potential of investing one's life in the lives of the lost and hopeless.

Brother Miguel Olivares is a young minister in his thirties and is the missions director for the First Baptist Church of Huejutla. He, his mother, Clementina, brothers Cristóbal and Marco, and sister Maricela are testimonies to the spirit of giving that enables missionaries to reach the hearts of desperate people.

Brother Miguel met the Johnsons at age seven. Fatherless and penniless, he had very little hope for the future. Neither did his mother, who was expecting her fourth child and facing enormous financial difficulty.

As Miguel and his siblings got to know the Johnson children, friendships began to develop and the door for witness was opened. The Johnsons were awaiting this opportunity. They responded with spiritual and material help and the personal touch that the love of the Lord always shows. Mrs. Johnson sewed a school uniform for little Maricela, and Clementina was invited to work in the Johnson home to help provide the needs of her family.

Miguel accepted Christ at the age of eight. He committed himself to service while suffering from severe epileptic seizures. The Lord healed his body, and he has not experienced a seizure since the age of twelve. In his youth Miguel allowed other priorities to take precedence over his commitment to the Lord. Brother Johnson was praying diligently about his spiritual condition. One afternoon he sent word by Clementina to Miguel inviting him to attend a meeting that evening in which they could pray about the Lord's call on Miguel's life. Miguel reluctantly attended the meeting; but while he was there the Lord touched his heart, and he realized that God was calling him to preach. Brother Johnson enrolled Miguel in Bible studies and began to carry him on mission trips that would provide him the experience he needed to grow in his calling.

Today Brother Miguel Olivares reveres Brother Buddy Johnson as the father he never had, and he praises the Lord for what He has done for his family. Giving truly pays great dividends in transformed lives!

So often we view God's power to reach the lost in distant lands with such limited perspective. David Dickson shares a testimony of how the Lord reached the heart of a Garífuna brother in Christ. The staff of Lifeword had produced taped copies of the Garífuna programs that were being broadcast on Radio Belize. Whether Pedro, a young man in his twenties, became interested simply because of his fascination with the technology of tapes or for some other reason is irrelevant. It is sufficient that the Holy Spirit had a plan. Pedro began listening to the tapes and asked to make copies of particular programs to listen to again. After exchanging tapes for a period of time, he suddenly announced to Brother Dickson that he had been convinced of his need for Christ. True to his word, he appeared in the church service that very night, responded to the invitation, and accepted Christ.

In a subsequent service, Brother Dickson noticed that Pedro remained in his seat toward the back of the building after everyone else had left. His head was bowed, and he was obviously very troubled. Brother Dickson sat down beside him and asked what was wrong. Pedro broke into sobs and was unable to control his voice for a while. When he finally was able to speak, he stated so simply a truth that we often fail to emphasize, "God really has suffered for us!" Brother Dickson observed that we would do well to remind ourselves often of the power of the basics, the simple truths of God's love for us. That truth is a powerful incentive to put His love into action!

Reflect, Discuss & Apply

1. How can you begin to share all of your resources including time, ability, and money with the cause of missions?

   _____
   _____
   _____

2. How can you cultivate a biblical perspective of your money's value and use?

   _____

3. How can you become a better advocate to your family and church of the importance of missions work?

4. What can you do to financially support the work of those who have been called as missionaries?

5. How can you develop sacrificial giving?

6. What can you do to make your giving a priority, as if your offering were the one that brought the gospel to your own ears?

7. Read missionaries' articles watching for accounts when God supplied a need in missions work. Ask the Lord to give you opportunities to help supply needs.
8. Read Philippians 4:19. How can you commit to be among the Lord's suppliers of the needs of missionaries?

9. Read 2 Corinthians 9:7; Luke 12:34; Malachi 3:10. How can you resolve to reap the joy of giving to the cause of missions?

12

BY GOD'S SUPREMACY OVER WORLD CONDITIONS

History is replete with accounts of the fervent spread of the gospel in times of world crisis, suffering, or catastrophe. During those times believers seized the moment of need to share the hope of the gospel. Many humbled themselves, admitted their helpless condition, and accepted Jesus as personal Savior.

People tend to become satisfied in times of prosperity and peace. Then satisfaction seems inevitably to deteriorate into mediocrity and spiral downward into moral and spiritual decay. Believers' lack of vigilance facilitates rampant spiritual decline. Jesus tried to warn us of such a state of affairs when He admonished us that we are salt and light to the world. If we do not season society with His precepts and shine as beacons of His truths, then the world is free to drift aimlessly into the chaos that sin always breeds. We have been called as missionaries in such a time.

We are blessed to have wise and experienced believers among us who have lived through previous world crises and can assure us that surrender to the Lord's call brings deliverance. Times of world crisis, such as the events of September 11, 2001, often create hearts which are softened and fertile for sowing gospel seed.

The writer of Hebrews offers encouragement for such times as these, *"Wherefore seeing we also are compassed about with so great a cloud of witnesses, let us* lay aside every weight, and the sin which doth so easily beset us, and let us run with patience the race that is set before us, looking unto Jesus the author and finisher of our faith; who for the joy that was set before him endured the cross, despising the shame, and is set down at the right hand of God" (Hebrews 12:1-2). Just before giving this great charge to believers the writer had delivered the great chapter of faith in which he challenged us to choose, as Moses did, the path of Christ. Certainly this path will be a journey in which we will know *"the reproach of Christ"* (Hebrews 11:26). By that choice we elect to *"suffer affliction with the people of God"* (verse 25).

On the other hand, choosing the path of Christ entitles us to the wonderful promise Paul shared, *"Who shall separate us from the love of Christ? shall tribulation, or distress, or persecution, or famine, or nakedness, or peril, or sword? As it is written, For thy sake we are killed all the day long; we are accounted as sheep for the slaughter. Nay, in all these things we are more than conquerors through him that loved us. For I am persuaded, that neither death, nor life, no angels, nor principalities, nor powers, nor things present, nor things to come, nor height, nor depth, nor any other creature, shall be able to separate us from the love of God, which is in Christ Jesus our Lord"* (Romans 8:35-39).

After speaking eloquently of keeping the commandments God has given us, John reminds us of the certainty of ultimate victory, *"For whatsoever is born of God overcometh the world: and this is the victory that overcometh the world, even our faith"* (1 John 5:4). What wonderful promises we can share with those whom we win to Christ!

We must not turn back; we must not turn aside. We must win souls all around us and around the world. Because the Lord touched my life in such a real way on the mission field in Uruguay so many years ago, I cannot forget that truth. If I could, I would not choose to forget for all the world.

How could I have known as I strained my eyes for my first glimpse of Uruguay from the rail of the ship on that evening in March, 1965, that I was about to be given a precious gift from the Lord, an experience that would forever mold my view of what is really important in life? It is true that I have many memories, though most of my keepsakes have long since faded. But my experience in Uruguay is not about the past. Because, far more important than memories, I was given a burden that is ever new and fresh. The desire to see Uruguayan souls saved is not about the past. It is about right now, and it's about the future.

Many times I watched my dad and the Uruguayan pastors pray for impossible victories in those four humble churches. Then I would watch the answers come stamped with the unmistakable hand of the Lord. In later years, when Satan would have destroyed every trace of BMAA missions in Uruguay, the light simply refused to go out. It was kept burning by the grace of almighty God, through daily prayer, and by the nurture of consecrated people committed to the salvation of souls however difficult the task. That is the formula for missions, and it works because it is God's plan.

The call rings out from Matthew 28. Time is of the essence. The human cry for spiritual hope is desperate. The consequences are eternal. The questions that we must face about carrying the gospel are:

If not now, then when?
If not you and I, then who?
Missions truly is the very heart of God!

Reflect, Discuss & Apply

1. Read John 16:33. How can you claim this promise in your life?

2. Read the prayer of Jesus in John 17. How can you use this prayer to encourage others?

3. What can you do to reassure missionaries that they can count you among their faithful prayer warriors?

4. Visualize the moment described in Revelation 20:15. How can you cultivate a personal attitude of critical urgency regarding missions outreach and the salvation of souls?

5. How can you express your thanksgiving to the Lord that He has given you the wonderful privilege of carrying the gospel to the world?